Sound Doctrine

Buddy Cobb

Sound Doctrine

Buddy Cobb

1454 Forest Glen Rd.
Abbeville, GA 31001-9621
USA
e-mail: buddyc@surfsouth.com

Cover by Osvaldo Lara
Layout by Martha C. Jaramillo R.

Bible quotations are from the King James Version.

This book may be freely duplicated for non-profit use.

ISBN 0-931221-50-1

Colombia para Cristo
P.O. Box 400
Moore Haven, FL 33471
USA
e-mail: rms05001@neutel.com.co

Printed in Colombia
2002

Contents

Preface

In Matthew 13, Jesus, using parables to describe what the kingdom of heaven would be like between His first coming and His second coming, said this in Verse 33:

> *The kingdom of heaven is like unto **leaven** which a woman took and hid in three measures of meal, till the whole was leavened.*

Leaven in scripture is symbolic of error. This can be seen by such scriptures as in Mt. 16:6:

> *Then Jesus said unto them, Take heed and beware of the **leaven** of the Pharisees and of the Sadducees.*

At first the disciples did not understand what Jesus was talking about, but after Jesus explained, in verse 12 we read:

> *Then understood they how that He bade them not beware of the leaven of bread, but of the **doctrine** of the Pharisees and of the Sadducees.*

The apostle Paul, speaking on the subject of leaven in I Co. 5:6-8, concludes with this in verse 8:

> *Therefore let us keep the feast, not with old leaven, neither with the leaven of malice and wickedness: but with the unleavened bread of sincerity and **truth**.*

We can see how leaven was used by both Jesus and

Paul as a symbol of false doctrine! The three measures of meal are speaking of the three levels of truth that are referred to in the scriptures as milk, bread, and meat (I Co. 3:2; He. 5:12, 13; Jo. 6:32-35,   I Co. 10:16, 17). The woman is symbolic of the church. Paul, speaking to Timothy and warning him about this very thing in II Ti. 4:3, 4 says:

> *For the time will come when they will not en-*
> *dure sound doctrine; but after their own lusts*
> *shall they heap upon themselves teachers, hav-*
> *ing itching ears; and they shall turn away their*
> *ears from the truth, and shall be turned to fables.*

Part I
Salvation Vs. Eternal Salvation

In II Tim. 2:15, the apostle Paul advises Timothy to...

*Study to show thyself approved unto God, a workman that needeth not to be ashamed, **rightly dividing the word of truth.***

In II Tim. 3:15, Paul reminds Timothy...

*And that from a child thou hast known the holy scriptures which are able to make thee **wise unto salvation** through faith which is **in Christ Jesus.***

Then in II Tim. 4:3, 4, Paul warns Timothy...

*For the time will come when they will not endure sound doctrine; but after their **own lusts** shall they heap to themselves teachers, having itching ears; and they shall turn away their ears from the truth, and shall be **turned unto fables.***

When Paul wrote Timothy about showing himself approved unto God, a workman that needed not to be **ashamed,** he also stated what was essential to that end: **the rightly dividing of the word of truth!** (Note: This would have to be the Old Testament scripture of which Paul was referring, as the New Testament was not yet in existence.) In his letter to Timothy it is evident that Paul was concerned about two things: first, that Timothy be **sound in doctrine** (what he taught), and second that he be **upright in his walk!** We see these two concerns also expressed in I Tim. 4:16, where Paul tells Timothy...

> *Take heed unto **thyself**, and unto the **doctrine**;*
> *continue in them: for in doing this thou shalt*
> *both save thyself and **them that hear thee**.*

That Timothy was born again and had also received the Holy Spirit is clear by what Paul says in II Tim. 1:5-7:

> *When I call to remembrance the **unfeigned faith**
> that is in thee, which dwelt first in thy grand-
> mother Lois, and thy mother Eunice; and **I am
> persuaded that in thee also**. Wherefore I put thee
> in remembrance that thou stir up **the gift of God**,
> which is in thee by the putting on of my hands:
> For God hath not given us **the spirit** of fear; but
> **of power, and of love, and of a sound mind**.*

It is also evident by what Paul wrote in II Tim. 1:9, 10, that he believed both he and Timothy were saved.

> ***Who hath saved us**, and called us with an holy
> calling, **not according to our works**, but accord-
> ing to his own purpose **and grace**, which was
> given us in Christ Jesus before the world be-
> gan, But is now made manifest by the appear-
> ing of our Saviour Jesus Christ, who **hath abol-
> ished death**, and hath brought **life and immor-
> tality** to light through the gospel:*

If Paul believed that he and Timothy were already saved, why then does he tell Timothy to "take heed unto thyself and unto the doctrine; continue in them: for on doing this thou shall both **save thyself** and **those who hear thee?**" Why would Timothy still need to be saved? Why would it require that he both be sound in doctrine and upright in his walk? Had not Paul just acknowledged that God had saved them and called them with an holy calling, not according **to their own works**, but according to **His own purpose and grace?**

Why would Paul tell Timothy to "fight the good fight of faith, lay hold on **eternal life**" (1 Tim. 6:12), if, in deed, he already had **eternal life** by virtue of being born again? The fact that we do have **eternal life** by our believing on the name of the Son of God is clear in 1 John 5:13.

> *These things have I written unto you that believe on the name of the Son of God, that ye may know that ye have eternal life, and that ye may believe on the name of the Son of God.*

It is the purpose of this teaching to answer the above questions **by rightly dividing the word of truth.**

In 1 Co. 15:22, the apostle Paul explains: *For as in Adam all die, even so in Christ shall all be made alive.* When Adam hearkened to the voice of his wife (Gen. 3:17) and ate of the tree of which God had commanded him to not eat, he sinned and died! When he died, because we were all in the loins of Adam, **we all died in him!**

> *Wherefore, as by one man **sin** entered into the world, and **death by sin;** and so **death** passed upon all men, for that all have sinned...* (Rom. 5:12)

Because of Adam's transgression (sin), we are born into this world **dead in trespasses and sins.** The only way out of this state is for God in His mercy and love to deliver us.

> *But, God, who is rich in mercy, for his great love wherewith he loved us, Even when we were **dead in sins,** hath quickened us together with Christ, (**by grace ye are saved.**)* (Ep. 2:4, 5)

It is obvious that the death spoken of in the above scriptures is not physical death but spiritual death. The life that Adam lost was the life that God had breathed into him, when He formed him from the dust of the ground.

*And the Lord God formed man of the dust of the ground and breathed into his nostrils **the breath of life;** and man became **a living soul.*** (Gen. 2:7)

In Job 32:8 we read, "But there is a spirit in man: and the inspiration (breath) of the Almighty giveth them understanding." When Adam lost this **breath of life**, he was no longer a living soul! The light (life) in his candle (spirit) went out!

Yea, the light of the wicked shall be put out, and the spark of his fire shall not shine. The light shall be dark in his tabernacle, and his candle shall be put out with him. (Job 18:5, 6)

Obviously the kind of light referred to here is spiritual, not natural. In order for one to walk in the way of God, they must have the light (understanding) of His way in them. Man without the Spirit of God in him is altogether void of this light.

*O Lord, I know that **the way of man is not in himself:** it is not in man that walketh to direct his steps.* (Je. 10:23)

There are only two ways that man can walk—his own way and **God's way.** God has made clear in the scriptures that His way is not our way.

For my thoughts are not your thoughts, neither are your ways my ways, saith the LORD. For as the heavens are higher than the earth, so are my ways higher than your ways, and my thoughts than your thoughts. (Is. 55:8, 9).

In Ps. 145:17 *we read:* **"The Lord is righteous in all his ways and holy in all his works."**

To depart then from His ways is <u>to walk in the ways of the wicked, whose works are evil!</u>

When Adam and Eve through an **evil heart** of unbelief departed from the living God, they left the paths of uprightness to walk in the ways of darkness (Pv. 2:13). It was **now** no longer possible for them to worship God **in spirit and in truth,** for they had changed **the truth of God into a lie!**

*Because that, when they knew God, they glorified Him not as God, neither were thankful; but became vain in their imaginations, and their foolish heart was **darkened. Who changed the truth of God into a lie,** and worshipped and served the creature more than the Creator, who is blessed for ever. Amen.* (Ro. 1:21, 25).

Adam, having been formed from the dust of the ground, was by nature, earthy (Ge. 2:7; I Co. 15:47)! As such he was corruptible (i.e. he could be tempted with evil). Therefore, he was subject to **sin and spiritual death!** The reason God had made man so <u>imperfect</u> in himself is revealed to us in II Co. 1:9.

*But we had the sentence of death in ourselves that **we should not trust in ourselves, but in God which raiseth the dead:***

The purpose of God in breathing the breath of life into Adam was to enable Adam to live in the Spirit and to be taught of God.

For what man knoweth the things of a man, save the spirit of man which is in him? Even so the things of God knoweth no man, but the spirit of

*God. Now we have received, not the spirit of
the world, but **the spirit which is of God;** that
we might know the things that are freely given
to us of God. Which things also we speak, not
in the words which man's wisdom teacheth, **but
which the Holy Ghost teacheth; comparing
spiritual things with spiritual.** But the natural
man receiveth not the things of the Spirit of God:
for they are foolishness unto him: neither can
he know them, **because they are spiritually dis-
cerned.*** (I Co. 2:11-14).

As long as Adam kept his trust in the living God,
walked in the Spirit, and did only what God commanded
him, he was clothed in **the righteousness of God.** The
imperfection in himself- **the shame of his nakedness-**
was not seen. Since all the treasures of wisdom and
knowledge are in God (Col. 2:3), the lack of knowing
how to direct his own steps was not a problem; all he
had to do was ask God.

*If any of you lack wisdom, let him ask of God,
that giveth to all men liberally, and upbraideth
not; and it shall be given him.* (James -1:5)

As long as Adam was content to abide under the
shadow of the Almighty God, he would be delivered
from evil and preserved blameless. God, by His Spirit,
would <u>lead him on to perfection.</u> Though Adam was
subject to death (losing life in the spirit), God would
<u>save him from death</u> until he was **changed** and **death
was swallowed up in victory!**

*Behold, I show you a mystery; we shall not all
sleep, but **we shall all be changed,** in a moment,
in the twinkling of an eye, at the last trump: for
the trumpet shall sound, and the dead shall be*

*raised incorruptible, and we **shall be changed**.
For this corruptible must put on incorruption,
and this mortal must put on immortality. So
when this corruptible shall have put on incorruption, and this mortal shall have put on immortality, then shall be brought to pass the saying that is written, **Death is swallowed up in
victory.*** (I Co. 15:51-54).

Until this final victory over death, Adam needed to
be <u>saved from death</u>. Though Adam was alive, until he
was changed from being corruptible to incorruptible,
from being mortal to immortal, he was subject to death.
There was only one that could save him from death—
GOD! God made it clear to Adam that the day in which
he disobeyed His voice (commandment), **he would
surely die!**

*And the Lord God **commanded** the man, saying, Of every tree of the garden thou mayest
freely eat: but of the tree of the knowledge of
good and evil, thou shalt not eat of it: for in the
day that thou eatest thereof thou shalt **surely
die.*** (Ge. 2:16, 17).

God was teaching from the beginning that **obedience to His voice** was essential to keeping God-given
Spirit life **unto life eternal!**

*He that loveth his life shall lose it; and he that
hateth his life in this world shall keep it **unto
life eternal.*** (Jo. 12:25)

Instead of holding to what God had told him and
keeping his trust in the living God, Adam harkened to
the voice of his wife and transgressed God's commandment! (Ge. 3:17). It is shown in II Cor. 11:3, that Eve was
beguiled by the serpent in her disobedience.

But I fear, lest by any means, as the serpent be-guiled Eve through his subtilty, so your minds should be corrupted from the simplicity that is in Christ.

Adam, however, was not deceived in his transgres-sions as shows in I Tim 2:14. "And Adam **was not de-ceived,** but the woman being deceived was in the trans-gression." God was showing by their example that, de-ceived or not, when we fail to believe (hearken to His word) and take our own way in the matter (trust in our-selves) we go astray! That is, we leave the paths of uprightness to walk in the ways of darkness! (Pv. 2:13) It also reveals that there is <u>no fear of God before our eyes.</u>

*The transgression of the wicked saith within my heart, that there is **no fear of God before his eyes.*** (Ps. 36:1)

Eve was not deceived concerning <u>what God had said</u> would happen if they ate of the tree. She told the ser-pent what God had said.

*And the woman said unto the serpent, We may eat of the fruit of the trees of this garden: But of the fruit of the tree which is in the midst of the garden, God hath said, Ye shall not eat of it, neither shall ye touch it, **lest ye die.*** (Ge. 3:3, 4)

Where Eve was deceived was in believing **the doc-trine** of the serpent.

*And the serpent said unto the woman, **Ye shall not surely die:** For God doth know that in the day ye eat thereof, then your eyes shall be opened, and ye shall be as gods, knowing good and evil.* (Ge. 3:4, 5)

The purpose of the serpent was to take away, if he

could, **the fear of God.** If he could get the woman (a figure of the church) to believe that she would **not really die,** then she would not be afraid to transgress! The reason God allowed the serpent to be in the garden is understood by what Jesus said to Simon Peter regarding him.

> *And the Lord said, Simon, Simon, behold, Satan hath desired to have you, that he may sift you as wheat: But I have prayed for thee, that **thy faith fail not:** and when thou art converted, strengthen thy brethren.* (Lu. 22:31, 32)

This was the trial of their faith! Job 26:13 tells us that God's hand formed the crooked serpent. The serpent is also called the devil or Satan, as shown in Re. 12:9.

> *And the great dragon was cast out, that old serpent, called the Devil, and Satan, which deceiveth the whole world: he was cast out into the earth, and his angels were cast out with him.*

We can then understand that God formed the crooked serpent to test His people. The purpose of the test is to reveal what is **in the heart,** whether or not we will keep His commandments! The reason that this is a **heart** matter is because it is **the test of love!** In Jo. 14:31 Jesus said: *"That the world may know that **I love the Father;** as the Father gave me **commandment, even so I do."*** In II Jo. 6 *the apostle John says, And **this is love** that we walk after **His commandments.** This is the commandment, That as ye have heard from the beginning, ye should walk in it.*

Again in Deu. 8:1, 2 Moses, speaking to the children of Israel, said...

> *All the commandments which I command thee*

*this day shall ye observe to do, that ye may live,
and multiply, and go in and possess the land
which the* LORD *sware unto your fathers.*

And thou shalt remember all the way which the
LORD *thy God led thee these forty years in the
wilderness to humble thee, and to prove to thee,
to know what was in thine heart ,whether thou
wouldest keep **his commandments, or no.***

We can see how the keeping of God's commandments is essential to the keeping of God-given **Spirit
life unto life everlasting!** Jesus in Jo. 12:50 said: *"And I
know that His commandment is life everlasting..."* Thus,
in Ecc. 12:13, 14 we read:

*Let us hear the conclusion of the whole matter:
Fear God, and keep His commandments: for
this is the whole duty of man. For God shall
bring **every work into judgment,** with every se-
cret thing, whether it be **good,** or whether it be
evil.*

It is clear by Eve's example what happens when one
doubts the truth of God's word and believes the lie (doctrine) of the Devil: *"You shall not surely die!"* When
Eve bought that line, she changed **the truth of God
into a lie** and was not afraid to transgress what she knew
God had said.

*And the serpent said unto the woman, **Ye shall
not surely die:** For God doth know that in the
day ye eat thereof, then your eyes shall be
opened, and ye shall be as gods, knowing good
and evil. And when the woman saw that the tree
was good for food, and that it was pleasant to
the eyes, and a tree to be desired to make one
wise, she took of the fruit thereof, and did eat,*

*and gave also unto her husband with her; and
he did eat.* (Ge. 3:4-6)

We see in this how the Devil comes as an angel of
light (II Co. 11:14) and how God uses him to test what is
in **the heart.** We can also see how, as *the disputer of
this world* (I Co. 1:20), God uses Satan to give us a choice
of believing the **truth** (what God says) or believing a
lie (what the disputer of this world says). In James 1:12-
15 we read,

> *Blessed is the man that **endureth temptation:**
> for when he is tried, he shall receive **the crown
> of life,** which the Lord hath promised to them
> that love **him.** Let no man say when he is
> tempted, I am tempted of God: for God cannot
> be tempted with **evil,** neither tempteth he any
> man: But every man is tempted, when he is
> drawn away of his own lust, and enticed. Then
> when lust hath conceived, it bringeth forth **sin:**
> and **sin,** when it is finished, **bringeth forth death.***

This is the graphic lesson that God purposed to teach
us from the beginning. **Blessed is the man that
endureth temptation!** For only <u>after he is tried</u> shall he
receive **the crown of life.** (i.e. eternal life), which God
has **reserved** for those <u>who love him</u>. When Adam and
Eve **failed the test of love,** here is what happened,

> *Because that, when they knew God, they glori-
> fied him not as God, neither were thankful; but
> became vain in their imaginations, and their
> foolish heart was darkened. Professing to **them-
> selves to be wise**, they became fools, and
> changed the glory of the incorruptible God into
> an image made like to corruptible man, and to
> birds, and four-footed beasts, and creeping*

*things. Wherefore God also gave them up to
uncleanness **through the lust** of their own
hearts, to dishonour their own bodies between
themselves: **Who changed the truth of God into
a lie, and worshipped and served the creature
more than the Creator,** who is blessed for ever.
Amen.* (Ro. 1:21-25)

Adam and Eve had now entered **the way of the
wicked!** They chose to go for **gain** instead of **godliness,** to serve **the creature** rather than **the Creator!**
As we noted before in the book of Job, we read...

*Yea, the light of the wicked shall be put out, and
the spark of his fire shall not shine. The light
shall be dark in his tabernacle, and his candle
shall be put out with him.* (Job. 18:5, 6)

In other words, Adam and Eve lost their access to
the truth. They no longer had spiritual understanding
but were now <u>carnally minded</u> **sold under sin!** They
could no longer walk in the light as children of light but
had now become darkness! They were no longer clothed
in the **righteousness of God** but were now **naked!**

*And the eyes of them both were opened, and **they
knew that they were naked;** and they sewed fig
leaves together, and made themselves aprons.*
(Ge. 3:7)

When Adam and Eve sewed fig leaves together to
use as a covering for their nakedness, it was to foreshadow the church, under Moses, electing to cover her-
self by <u>the works of the law.</u> For God in time under the
leadership of Moses would bring His people out of Egypt
unto Himself at Mount Sinai. There He would offer to
restore them back into a **hearing** relationship with Himself. They, however, for **the fear of losing their life,**

would draw back from hearing God's voice and elect instead to hear Moses' voice!

> *And they said unto Moses, Speak thou with us, and we will hear: but let not God speak with us,* ***lest we die.*** (Ex.20:19)

God went along with their request and used Moses as a mediator between Himself and the people to establish them under the covenant of the law. This was essential to God's plan and purpose. Before God would provide a way for man to be redeemed from under <u>the law of sin and death,</u> He first needed to use <u>the law of God</u> as a school master to teach some great lessons. Let us look now at those lessons.

There are four kinds of trees spoken of in the Garden of Eden. They are there as a figure of <u>the four kinds of lives</u> that are possible for us to experience. The fact that God uses trees in scriptures as a figure of men's lives in shown in Deu. 20:19.

> *When thou shalt besiege a city a long time, in making war against it to take it, thou shalt not destroy* ***the trees*** *thereof by forcing an ax against them: for thou mayest eat of them, and thou shalt not cut them down (**for the tree of the field is man's life**) to employ them in the siege:*

In Genesis 2:9 we read...

> *And out of the ground made the LORD God to grow every* ***tree*** *that is* ***pleasant to the sight, and good for food;*** *the* ***tree of life*** *also in the midst of the garden, and the* ***tree of knowledge of good and evil.***

The first kind of tree mentioned, the one which is **pleasant to the sight and good for food,** represents

life in the Spirit. This life is what Adam had in the beginning and is described in grater detail in Ps. 1:1-3.

> *Blessed is the man that walketh not in the counsel of the ungodly, nor standeth in the way of sinners, nor sitteth in the seat of the scornful. But his delight is in the law of the LORD; and in his law doth he meditate day and night. And **he shall be like a tree** planted by the rivers of water, that bringeth forth his fruit in his season; his leaf also shall not wither; and whatsoever he doeth shall prosper.*

The second tree mentioned, **the tree of life,** represents incorruptible, immortal, resurrection life! This tree is spoken of on greater detail in Re. 22:1-2.

> *And he showed me a pure river of water of life, clear as crystal, proceeding out of the throne of God and of the Lamb. In the midst of the street of it, and on either side of the river was there **the tree of life**, which bare twelve manner of fruits, and yielded her fruit every month: and **the leaves of the tree** were for **the healing of the nations.***

Once God has brought His true people forth out from among the dead by resurrection into incorruptible, immortal life (perfection), He will then use them as the mountain of the Lord's house for **the healing of the nations**.

> *And it shall come to pass in the last days, that the mountain of the Lord's house shall be established in the top of the mountains, and shall be exalted above the hills; and **all nations shall flow unto it**. And many people shall go and say,*

*Come ye, and let us go up to the mountain of the
LORD, to the house of the God of Jacob; and **he
will teach us his ways, and we will walk in his
paths:** for out of Zion shall go forth the law, and
the word of the LORD from Jerusalem. And he
shall judge among the nations, and shall rebuke
many people: and they shall beat their swords
into plowshares, and their spears into
pruninghooks: nation shall not lift up sword
against nation, neither shall they learn war any
more.* (Is. 2:2-4).

The third tree mentioned in the garden is **the tree of
the knowledge of good and evil.** This is the only tree
which God commanded that Adam and Eve were not to
eat of because it represented **life after the flesh.** In the
book of Galatians the apostle Paul explains about the
flesh.

*This I say then, **Walk in the Spirit,** and ye shall
not fulfil the lust of **the flesh.** For **the flesh** lusteth
against **the Spirit,** and **the Spirit** against **the
flesh:** and these are contrary the one to the
other: so that ye cannot do the things that ye
would.* (Ga. 5:16, 17).

***Be not deceived;** God is not mocked: for what-
soever a man soweth, that shall he also reap.
For he that soweth to **his flesh** shall of **the flesh
reap corruption;** but he that soweth to **the Spirit**
shall of **the Spirit reap life everlasting.*** (Ga. 6:7,
8).

It is because of this law of sowing and reaping and
the fact that man is a partaker of flesh and blood, that
man has **the sentence of death** in himself. It is clear
that to avoid spiritual death (i.e. losing the ability to

live godly), man must not live after **the flesh!** It was true in the garden and it is true today!

> *Therefore, brethren, we are debtors, not to the flesh, to live after the flesh.* *For **if ye live after the flesh, ye shall die,** but if ye through **the Spirit** do mortify the deeds of the body, **ye shall live.*** (Ro. 8:12-13)

The definition of **spiritual death and life** is revealed to us in Ro. 8:6 where we read, *"For to be carnally minded is death; but to be spiritually minded is life and peace."* The reason that Adam and Eve took the way of the flesh was that they perceived they would **gain** by doing so. In the pursuit of personal **gain** they lost **godliness.** God would use their **error** to teach the great truth that **godliness with contentment is great gain.**

> *If any man teach otherwise, and consent not to wholesome words, even the words of our Lord Jesus Christ, and to the doctrine which is according to **godliness;** he is proud, knowing nothing, but doting about questions and strifes of words, whereof cometh envy, strife, railings, evil surmisings, perverse disputings of men of corrupt minds, and destitute of **the truth, supposing that gain is godliness: from such withdraw thyself. But godliness with contentment is great gain.*** (I Tim. 6:3-6)

Once Adam and Eve were drawn away of their own lust and enticed, when lust conceived it brought forth **sin and death** (James 1:14, 15)! Adam and Eve were no longer in the liberty of the law of the spirit of life (Ro. 8:1, 2). They were now **in the bondage of corruption** under the law of sin and death.

> *Wherefore, as by one man sin entered into the*

world, and death by sin; and so death passed
upon all men, for that all have sinned: For un-
til the law sin was in the world: but sin is not
imputed when there is no law. Nevertheless
death reigned from Adam to Moses, even over
them that had not sinned after the similitude of
Adam's transgression, **who is the figure of him**
that was to come. (Ro. 5:12-14).

As we have noted, the fourth kind of tree in the garden was **the fig tree.** We know that this tree was there
by the fact that Adam and Eve used its leaves to make
themselves a covering for their nakedness. In so doing,
as we have also noted, they were foreshadowing **the**
next error that God's people would make, that is, of
trying to establish their own righteousness (i.e. perfect
themselves) by **the work of the law.** While the law
would give them an outer covering (leaves), it would
leave them without the fruit, i.e. **life of the Spirit!** We
are given more details on the fig tree in Mark 11:12-14.

And on the marrow, when they were come from
Bethany, he was hungry: And seeing a **fig tree**
afar off having **leaves,** *he came, if haply he might*
find anything thereon: and when he came to it,
he found **nothing but leaves;** *for the time of figs*
was not yet. And Jesus answered and said unto
it, No man eat fruit of thee hereafter for ever.
And his disciples heard it.

Thus, in the four kinds of trees in the garden, we
have pictured for us the four kinds of men's lives that
man can experience.

First, **life in the Spirit** is <u>where</u> in the liberty of the
Spirit we walk in obedience to God's voice, **the Living**
Word! <u>Where</u> under the covering of **the righteousness**

of God, we can have the shame of our nakedness (imperfection) covered and **be preserved blameless** until our **change comes, i.e. resurrection!** <u>Where</u> though we are alive, **we are subject to death,** until <u>death</u> is swallowed up in victory!

Second, **resurrection life** is <u>where</u> we are **changed** where corruptible puts on incorruption and mortal puts on immortality, and <u>death is swallowed up in victory!</u> Therefore, it is **eternal everlasting life, where we shall ever be with the Lord!**

Third, **life after the flesh,** is <u>where </u>we walk in disobedience to **the voice of God** after **the lust of our flesh, the lust of our eyes, and the pride of life** (I Jo. 2:16). <u>Where </u> in the pursuit of <u>gain</u> we lose <u>godliness</u> (life in the spirit) and are now naked, robbed of our covering (God's righteousness) **Cursed children** (II Pe. 2:14) who have forsaken the paths of righteousness , to walk in the ways of darkness, and are now in the bondage of corruption, under **the law of sin and death!**

Fourth, **life in the law** is <u>where</u> we walk after **the letter of God's written word.** <u>Where</u> we attempt to cover the shame of our nakedness (be justified) by **the works of the law and are going about** to establish our own righteousness. <u>Where</u> we have the form of godliness but deny **the power (Spirit life) thereof** (II Tim. 3:5)!

The order in which the trees are introduced in Genesis is significant, for God began by breathing **the breath of life** into Adam, that is, **freely** imparting to Adam **life in the Spirit.** This was, as we have seen, to enable Adam to be **taught of God,** for God had not put in man the way he should go (Jer. 10:23). Therefore, it is critical that Adam only did what God taught him to do if he was to **live and not die!** If Adam had honoured God as God and had refused to harken to another voice, he would have been kept by the wisdom and **power of God** (i.e. the Spirit of God), **through faith** (i.e. obedience to God's voice), unto **perfection** (i.e. resurrection)! Therefore, the second tree introduced was the **tree of life!** If Adam had been steadfast with God, then **sin and death** would never have had an opportunity to enter. Instead, as we know, he chose to hearken to the voice of the woman, **(his flesh)** and to partake of the third tree mentioned **the tree of the knowledge of good and evil!**

Once Adam and Eve, through **disbelief,** transgressed God's commandment and ate of **the tree of the knowledge of good and evil,** the eyes of them both were opened and they knew they were naked. To cover their nakedness, as we have seen, they sewed **fig leaves** together and made themselves aprons, thus foreshadowing that the people under Moses would elect to come under the covering of **the law.** Therefore, the fourth and final kind of tree spoken of in the garden is the **fig tree.** As we have noted, Jesus **cursed** the fig tree that had leaves but no fruit, as it was a figure of the church under the law.

> *For as many as are of the works of the law are under **the curse:** for it is written, **Cursed** is every one that continueth not in all things which are written in the book of the law to do them.* (Ga. 3:10).

Once Adam and Eve fell from the steadfastness with God, since all were in Adam, all fell with him! The man that God had created **in the image and glory of God** (I Co. 11:7) had now changed **the glory of the incorruptible God** into an image made like to **corrupt-**

ible man (Ro.1:23)! Though Adam had begun **in the Spirit and wisdom of God,** he had now become **foolish** to believe he could **be made perfect** by the flesh (Ga. 3:3)! God would use this error to teach…

> *It is the spirit that quickeneth; **the flesh profiteth nothing:** the words that I speak unto you, they are **spirit** and they are **life.** (Jo. 6:63).*

Fortunately, the fall (death) of Adam did not bring to an end God's purpose top bring man **up into perfection,** i.e. **resurrection life!** In fact, Adam's fall was essential to the way God had before ordained, that in the process of time He would work it out. For in the economy of God's plan, He purposed to reveal **the man of sin** before He would reveal **the man of righteousness,** i.e. **the perfect man, Christ!**

> *Now we beseech you, brethren, by the coming of our Lord Jesus Christ, and by our gathering together unto Him, that ye be not soon shaken in mind, or be troubled, neither by spirit, nor by word, nor by letter as from us, as that **the day of Christ** is at hand. Let no man deceive you by any means: for that day shall not come, except there come a falling away first, and that **man of sin** be revealed, the son of perdition; Who opposeth and exalteth himself above all that is called God, or that is worshipped; so that he **as God** sitteth in **the temple of God,** showing **himself** that **he is God.** (II Thes. 2:1-4)*

Since **the man of sin** operates in **the temple of God,** we need to let the scriptures identify for us **the temple of God.**

> *Know ye not that **ye are the temple of God,** and that **the Spirit of God** dwelleth in you? If any*

*man defile **the temple of God,** him shall God destroy; for **the temple of God** is holy, **which temple ye are.*** (1Co. 3:16-17)

*What? Know ye not that your body is **the temple of the Holy Ghost** which is in you, which ye have of God, and ye are not your own? For ye are bought with a price: therefore glorify God **in your body, and in your spirit, which are God's*** (1Co. 6:19,20)

*And what agreement hath **the temple of God** with idols? For **ye are the temple of the living God;** as God hath said, I will dwell in them, and walk in them; and I will be their God, and they shall be my people. Wherefore come out from among them, and be ye separate, saith the Lord, and touch not the unclean thing; and I will receive you, and I will be a Father unto you, and you shall be my sons and daughters, saith the Lord Almighty.* (2Co. 6:16-18)

We understand then by the above scriptures that it was in keeping with God's purpose that **the man of sin** be revealed first. Therefore, God would use the falling away of this first man (the first Adam), who was of the earth earthy, for this purpose. However, in the fullness of time God would send into the world **the second man, the last Adam, the Lord from heaven, the man of righteousness,** whom he would use as **the Savior!** He would redeem us and recover **all who would receive Him** out of the **flesh and alienation from the life of God (death),** into which the first Adam's disobedience got us. So that, once recovered from **so great death,** we might be led by the Spirit of God into all truth, **walk as children of the light, and go on to perfection!** How-

ever, now that man through disobedience was out of the
Spirit and in the flesh, walking in his own ways, God
would let him discover where such ways lead.

> *There is a way that seemeth right unto a man,*
> *but the end thereof are **the ways of death.*** (Pv.
> 14:12)

Now that Adam and Eve were out from under the
covering of God's Spirit, God Himself moved to provide them with another covering.

> *Unto Adam and to his wife did the* LORD *God*
> *make coats of skins, and clothed them.* (Ge. 3:21)

This was to foreshadow the animal sacrifice that God
would establish under the first covenant of the Law, i.e.
the Levitical priesthood. The law itself, in turn, would
be a shadow of a **perfect sacrifice** that would come!
For man could not be **made perfect** by the sacrifices
offered under the law.

> *For the law having a shadow of good things to*
> *come, and not the very image of the things, can*
> *never with those sacrifices which they offered*
> *year by year continually make the comers there-*
> *unto perfect.* (He. 10:1)

The next thing that God did was to make sure that
man would no longer have access to **the tree of life!**

> *And the* LORD *God said, Behold, the man is be-*
> *come as one of us, to know good and evil: and*
> *now, lest he put forth his hand, and take also of*
> ***the tree of life,** and eat, **and live forever.** There-*
> *fore the* LORD *God sent him forth from the Gar-*
> *den of Eden, **to till the ground** from whence he*
> *was taken. So he drove out the man; and he*
> *placed at the east of the garden of Eden*

*Cherubims, and a flaming sword which turned every way, to keep **the way of the tree of live.*** (Ge. 3:22-24)

Now that man was put out of the way of God he could no longer live in the paradise of God or eat of the tree of life, i.e. have access to eternal life! Man was now under the curse of God and no longer under His blessing.

*Thus saith the Lord: **Cursed** be the man that trusteth in man, and maketh **flesh his arm** and whose heart departeth from the Lord.* (Jer. 17:5)

The flaming sword guarding the way **of the tree of life** pictures for us the judgment that fallen man would have to come through before he could again have access to **the tree of life!** God would never allow man access to **eternal life** (the life of God) until he came to judgment, was back in a sound mind and properly covered (clothed) in **the righteousness of God!**

As we have noted, in the fullness of time God would send the second man, the last Adam, His **only begotten son, Jesus,** into the world as **the better sacrifice** to redeem fallen man. First, however, He would take four thousand years to show man that his own ways, i.e. the ways of the flesh, profits nothing.

There are two forms of the flesh in which corruptible man can be found. The first form God shows is the way of **the uncircumcised, the lawless, the Gentile.** The second is the **way of the circumcised, those under the law, the Jew.** To show the first, God sent man out of the garden to *plow the ground* from whence he was taken (Ge. 3:23). This was to show just what corruptible man is like when he rebels against the words of God, contemns the counsel of the most High and walks

instead in the counsel of the ungodly (hearkens to another voice). Now that man was no longer under the
covering of God's righteousness, God would let the
shame of his nakedness be manifest.

> *And God saw that the wickedness of man was
> great in the earth, and that every **imagination**
> of the thoughts of his heart was only **evil** con-
> tinually. The earth also was **corrupt** before God
> and the earth was filled with violence. And God
> looked upon the earth, and, behold, **it was cor-
> rupt** for all flesh had **corrupted his way** upon
> the earth. And God said unto Noah: The end of
> all flesh is come before me; **for the earth is filled
> with violence** through them; and, behold I will
> destroy them with the earth.* (Ge. 6:5, 11 -13)

So God brought His judgment upon the world of
the ungodly by bringing the flood! Only Noah and his
family were saved, thus making it an example unto all
who, after that time, **live ungodly!** What enabled Noah
to escape **the wrath of God** and to be saved is shown in
this scripture.

> ***By faith Noah,*** *being warned of God of **things
> not seen** as yet, moved with **fear,** prepared an
> ark to the saving of his house; by the which he
> condemned the world, and became **heirs of the
> righteousness which is by faith.*** (He. 11:7).

What enabled Noah to so move **by faith** is revealed
in Genesis 6:8. *But Noah found **grace** in the eyes of the
Lord.* By Noah's example God was showing that to escape **the wrath of God** in the time of judgment, one
must be found in <u>the righteousness of God, which is by
grace through faith!</u>

God, in the days of Noah, was setting forth some

very important lessons. First, He purposed to show His indignation and wrath (His severity) upon all that would <u>live ungodly,</u> and second, He wanted to show His <u>grace and kindness</u> (goodness) upon those that would fear Him and keep His commandments, i.e. **live godly** (Ro. 11:22)!

Thus, the first world (age) ended as it says in II Pe. 2:5. God *spared not the old world, but saved Noah the eighth person, a preacher of **righteousness**, bringing in the flood upon the world of **the ungodly.***

God had let it be seen that corruptible man in his natural state is nothing more than **a beast!**

> *I said in mine heart concerning the estate of the sons of men, that God might manifest them, and that they might see **that they themselves are beasts.** For that which befalleth the sons of men befalleth beasts; even one thing befalleth them: as the one dieth, so dieth the other; yea, they have all one breath; so that **a man hath no pre-eminence above a beast:** for all is vanity. All go unto one place; **all are of the dust, and all turn to dust again.*** (Ecc. 3:18-20)

God was also showing that though **we are His people** that apart from Him <u>we are wise to do evil,</u> but to do good we have no knowledge.

> ***For my people** is foolish, they have not known me; they are sottish children, and they have none understanding: **they are wise to do evil,** but **to do good they have no knowledge.** I beheld the earth, and, lo, it was without form, and void; and the heavens, and they had no light. I beheld the mountains, and, lo, they trembled, and all the hills moved lightly. I beheld, and, lo,*

there was no man, and all the birds of heaven
were fled. I beheld, and, lo, the fruitful place
was a wilderness, and all the cities thereof were
broken down at the presence of the LORD, and
by his fierce anger. For thus hath the LORD said,
*the whole land shall be desolate; yet will **I not***
make a full end. (Jer. 4:22-27)

Because the Lord God had spoken to the serpent in
the garden and said,

Thou art cursed above all cattle, and above ev-
ery beast of the field; upon thy belly shalt thou
*go, and **dust** shalt thou eat all the days of thy*
*life: And **I will put enmity between thee and***
the woman, and between thy seed and her seed;
*and it shall **bruise thy head** and thou shalt bruise*
his heel. (Gen. 3:14, 15)

To fulfil His word to the serpent, the Lord God had
to preserve a godly seed (Noah). He could not make a
full end! God would, in the process of time, bring forth
from the line of this godly seed another woman, **Israel.**
Out of this woman God would bring into the world the
promised seed, Christ, that would bruise the head of the
serpent! For the serpent had now gained by one man's
disobedience the **power of death** over all men! If God
was to ever take man on to perfection, He would now
have to first recover him from under **the power of death!**

Since man in the pursuit of his own perfection had
chosen to walk after the flesh **in the uncircumcision
thereof,** God had let it be seen just where that would
lead. Instead of taking him on **to perfection** it exposed
the shame of his nakedness and took him back to the
dust from whence he came!

After this, through the godly seed line of Noah, God

in the process of time brought forth Abraham and es-
tablished a covenant with him.

> *And God said unto Abraham, Thou shalt keep*
> *my covenant thereof, thou, and thy seed after*
> *thee in their generations. This is my covenant,*
> *which ye shall keep, between me and you and*
> *thy seed after thee; Every man child among you*
> *shall* ***be circumcised.*** (Ge. 17:9, 10)

God was ready to show the other form of the flesh
that corruptible man could walk in—the way of circumcision! In preparation for this instruction, God brought
Abraham and his natural prosperity into the covenant
of circumcision in the flesh. This would put a differ-
ence between the Jew, as they would later become
known, and the Gentile. When they had grown to be
about seventy-five in number, God led them down into
Egypt. There they multiplied in number, and after four
hundred years, God led them out under the hand of
Moses. Moses brought them to Mt. Sinai to meet with
God! There God made them this offer.

> *Now therefore, if ye will* ***obey my voice indeed,***
> *and keep my covenant, then ye shall be a pecu-*
> *liar treasure unto me above all people: for all*
> *the earth is mine:* (Ex. 19:5)

Thus, God offered them this opportunity to come
back under the authority of His Spirit so that He might
take them on to perfection. They, however, for fear of
losing their own life, replied...

> *And they said unto Moses, Speak thou with us,*
> *and we will hear: but* ***let not God speak with***
> ***us, lest we die.*** *And Moses said unto the people,*
> *Fear not: for God is come to prove you, and*

that his fear may be before your faces, *that ye
sin not.* (Ex. 20:19, 20)

God would show by their example that as long as
one fears losing their life, (i.e. love themselves and their
own life) more than they fear God, (i.e. love God and
His life), they cannot <u>lay hold of eternal life!</u>

He that loveth his life shall lose it; and he that
hateth his life in this world shall keep it *unto
life eternal.* (Jo. 12:25)

Their refusal to accept God's offer, however, did
not take God by surprise. He, of course, knew before-
hand that they would not accept His offer. Therefore,
He sent a deliverer, **Moses**, not **the redeemer Jesus,** to
bring them to Himself at Mt. Sinai.

All this was essential to God's plan to teach the next
lesson concerning the flesh, <u>the way of the circumcised!</u>
Since they refused God's offer of a personal hearing
relationship, God used Moses as **a mediator** between
Himself and the people to establish them under the first
covenant of the law. God purposed to accomplish several things by the law, **righteousness,** however, was not
one of them.

*Wherefore then serveth the law? It was added
because of transgressions, till **the seed** should
come to whom the promise was made; and it
was ordained by angels in the hand of **a mediator.** Now **a mediator** is not a mediator of one,
but God is one. Is the law then against the prom-
ises of God? God forbid: **for if there had been
a law given which could have given life,** verily
righteousness should have been by the law. But
the scripture hath concluded all under sin, that
the promise by faith of Jesus Christ might be*

*given to them that believe. But before faith came,
we were kept under the law, shut up unto the
faith which should afterwards be revealed.
Wherefore* **the law was our schoolmaster to
bring us unto Christ,** *that* **we might be justified
by faith.** (Ga. 3:19-24)

In the garden man sought <u>his own wisdom;</u> in the
wilderness man sought <u>his own righteousness.</u> Both
were man's attempts to be as God (i.e. made perfect) by
the works of his own hands! In the garden the man
hearkened to the voice of the woman (Eve.) In the wilderness the woman hearkened to the voice of the man
(Moses). The first took man in the way of <u>uncircumcision</u>
(the Gentile) and the second in the way of <u>circumcision</u>
(the Jew). God was using their error to teach the truth
that...

*Circumcision is nothing, and uncircumcision is
nothing, but* **the keeping of the commandments
of God.** (I Co. 7:19)

God was showing that it was not in man to know
the way he should go! That though there were ways
that seemed right unto him, they were the ways of darkness, not light, and that the ends thereof were death, not
life! Having taken four thousand years to teach man
that the flesh profiteth nothing, God was ready to send
into the world **the Redeemer,** <u>His only begotten Son,
Jesus!</u>

For God so loved the world that **he gave his
only begotten Son,** *that* **whosoever believeth in
him** *should not perish, but have* **everlasting life.**
(Jo. 3:16)

After so long a time, God was ready to open **The
Way** for man to be saved out of **death** and <u>the error of</u>

his own ways! Since the first Adam had sold us all under sin and death by one act of disobedience, the first step of recovery required **redemption!** This Jesus accomplished for us by the shedding of **His own blood, as He laid down His life in obedience to Father God!**

> *Neither by the blood of goats and calves, but **by his own blood** he entered in once into the holy place, having obtained **eternal redemption for us.** (He. 9:12)*

Under the law, as we have noted, God instituted animal sacrifice to foreshadow the truth that with the shedding of blood there could be forgiveness of sins. However, the problem was that those sacrifices could not make one perfect, because they still left the worshiper separated from God. This was because it was not possible for the blood of bulls and goats to take away sins.

> *For there is verily a disannulling of the commandment going before for the weakness and unprofitableness thereof. For the law made nothing perfect, but **the bringing in of a better hope did; by the which we draw nigh unto God.*** (He. 7:18, 19)

Once Jesus paid the wages of sin for us, God had a ransom!

> *For this is good and acceptable in the sight of God our Saviour; Who will have all men to be saved, and to come unto the knowledge of the truth. For there is one God, and **one mediator** between God and men, **the man Christ Jesus; Who gave himself a ransom for all,** to be testified in due time.* (I Tim. 2:3-6)

Once God had what He required for the taking away

of sins, **our ransom,** He could then restore us out form
under **the guilt and penalty of sin!** Having the conscience cleansed by the blood (He. 9:14) and released from
death, i.e. **quickened by the Spirit,** we can now be reconciled to God; and once reconciled, we can then **be
saved by HIS LIFE!**

> *For when we were yet without strength, in due
> time Christ died for the ungodly. For scarcely
> for a righteous man will one die: yet
> peradventure for a good man some would even
> dare to die. But God commendeth his love to-
> ward us, in that, while we were yet sinners,
> Christ died for us. Much more then, being now
> **justified by his blood,** we shall be saved from
> wrath through him. For if, when we were en-
> emies, we were **reconciled to God by death of
> his Son,** much more, **being reconciled, we shall
> be saved by his life.** (Ro. 5:6-10)*

After Jesus paid the price for our redemption, for it
to be beneficial at all, man would have to repent! That
is, he would have to turn from a walk after **the flesh,**
seeking his own wisdom and his own righteousness, to
walk after **the Spirit!** For only in **the way of the Spirit
of God** could man be led by the **wisdom of God,** be
clothed in **the righteousness of God,** and **live in the
Spirit (Life) of God!** It would be of no benefit to man
or God for God to forgive man his trespasses and sins,
cleanse him from all unrighteousness, and deliver his
soul from the power of darkness and death, if he was
not going to **walk after the Spirit in the light (Life) of
the living!** Therefore, repentance is God's first require-
ment on the part of man. Thus, John the Baptist was
sent by God as a special messenger to prepare the way
for Jesus.

> *As it is written in the prophets, Behold, I send
> my messenger before thy face, which shall pre-
> pare thy ways before thee. The voice of one cry-
> ing in the wilderness, Prepare ye the way of the
> Lord, make his paths straight. John did baptize
> in the wilderness, and preach* **the baptism of
> repentance for the remission of sins.** (Mk. 1:2-4)

When Jesus was ready to begin His ministry at the
age of thirty, even He came to John to be baptized into
the baptism of repentance.

> *Then cometh Jesus from Galilee to Jordan unto
> John, to be baptized of him. But John forbade
> Him, saying, I have need to be baptized of thee,
> and comest thou to me? And Jesus answering
> said unto him, Suffer it to be so now: for thus it
> becometh us* **to fulfil all righteousness.** *Then
> he suffered him.* (Mt. 3:13-15).

John did not understand why Jesus came to be baptized by him, for John knew that Jesus was <u>the Son of
God!</u> The **first man** (Adam) had come from the dust of
the earth. Though Jesus was in the world in fashion as
a man, He nonetheless was **the Lord from heaven and
had come from His Father, God!** However, Jesus had
now descended (Ep. 4:9, 10), that is, He had left the glory
that He had with the Father before the world was, where
He was in the form of God (Jo. 17:5) and had become a
partaker of <u>flesh and blood.</u> Thus, he was now in the
world, like Adam before Him, <u>in fashion as a man</u> (Ph.
2:8) and in the likeness of sinful flesh (Ro. 8:3)!

> *And* **the Word was made flesh,** *and dwelt among
> us, (and we beheld his glory, the glory as of* **the
> only begotten of the Father,**) *full of grace and
> truth.* (Jo. 1:14)

> *Forasmuch then as the children are partakers of **flesh and blood**, he also himself likewise **took part of the same**; that through death he might destroy him that had **the power of death, that is, the devil;** and deliver them who through fear of death were all their lifetime subject to bondage. For verily he took not on him the nature of angels; but **he took on him the seed of Abraham. Wherefore in all things it behoved him to be made like unto his brethren,** that he might be a **merciful and faithful high priest** in things pertaining to God, **to make reconciliation** for sins of the people. For in that he himself hath **suffered being tempted,** he is able to succour them that are tempted.* (He. 2:14-18)

In order for Jesus to be a merciful and faithful high priest, He needed to be compassed with the same infirmity that we are.

> *For every **high priest** taken from among men is ordained for men in things pertaining to God, that he may offer both gifts and sacrifices for sins: Who can have compassion on the ignorant, and on them that are out of the way; for that **he himself also is compassed with infirmity.*** (He. 5:1, 2)

In order for Jesus to be compassed with infirmity, it was necessary that He be a partaker of **flesh and blood.** That is, it was necessary for him to empty Himself of the glory that He had with the Father before the world was and to be in the world in the same weakness that we are, in the same <u>flesh nature with all of its lust and affections</u> so that He might be tempted the same as all men.

For we have not an high priest which cannot be
touched with the feeling of our infirmities; but
*was **in all points tempted like as we are,** yet*
without sin. (He. 4:15)

It was in preparation for His being tempted that Jesus
came to John to be baptized. Since Jesus was now in
the flesh, if He, as the second man and the last Adam (I
Co. 15:45), was going to avoid error of the first man, the
first Adam, He would have to stay out of **the way of the
flesh!** Now that He was in the flesh, it was just as true
for Him as it was for Adam before Him, that is, if **He
ever walked after the flesh** He would die in sin! Therefore, to be our redeemer and to put before us an example of **the way, the truth, and the life,** Jesus had to
stay out of sin and death! By keeping Himself in re-
straint and doing only those things that **the Spirit of
God** taught Him to do, would He succeed!

In submitting Himself to the baptism of repentance,
Jesus was doing two things. First, He repented of ever
walking after **the flesh in the lust thereof;** and second,
He set before us an example that we should follow in
His steps! For He had been sent not only to redeem us,
but also to show us how, while **in the weakness of the
flesh,** to fulfil **all righteousness and go on to perfection, i.e. immortality!**

And Jesus, when He was baptized, went up
straightway out of the water: and, lo, the heav-
*ens were opened unto him, and He saw **the Spirit***
***of God** descending like a dove, and lighting upon*
Him: And lo a voice from heaven, saying, This
is my beloved Son, in whom I am well pleased.
(Mt. 3:16, 17)

Receiving **the Spirit of God** was the next step necessary in **Jesus' fulfilling all righteousness.** For only as He walked <u>in the Spirit</u> would He not fulfil the lust of the flesh (Ga. 5:16)! Only by being led of <u>the Spirit of God</u> can one be clothed in the **right garment (the righteousness of God)** and be kept from **sin and death!** Now that Jesus was here as the second man and as the last Adam, He would have to succeed where the first Adam failed. Having submitted Himself to the baptism of repentance and having received the Holy Spirit, Jesus was ready for testing; that is, He was ready to be tried by the devil to see if He could be enticed and drawn away by His own lust!

> *Then was Jesus led up of the Spirit unto the wilderness to be tempted of the devil* (Mt. 4:1)

In order for Jesus to redeem us out of death, He would have to offer Himself to God, His Father, without spot (He. 9:14). This would require Jesus to take upon Himself the form of a servant (humble Himself) and become obedient unto death—<u>even the death of the cross!</u>

> *Forasmuch then as the children are partakers of **flesh and blood,** he also himself likewise took part of the same; that **through death** he might destroy him that had the power of death, that is, the devil;* (He. 2:14)

> *And being found in fashion as a man, he humbled himself, and became **obedient unto death,** even **the death of the cross.*** (Ph. 2:8)

> *And having spoiled principalities and powers, he made a show of them openly, triumphing over them in it.* (Col. 2:15)

By enduring the temptations that the devil put before him to entice Him and draw Him out from **the covering of the Spirit of God,** Jesus avoided the error of the first Adam. Therefore, when He came out of the wilderness, having spoiled the devil's attempt to draw Him out <u>through the lust of His flesh</u> unto **sin and death,** He came in <u>the power of the Holy Spirit</u> (Lu. 4:14)!

When He began His ministry, having gathered some followers, He began to address what we have seen to be the issues right from the beginning.

He said unto His disciples, Therefore I say unto you, Take no thought for your life, what ye shall eat, neither for the body, what ye shall put on. ***The life is more than meat, and the body is more than raiment.*** *Consider the ravens: for they neither sow nor reap; which neither have storehouse nor barn; and God feedeth them: how much more are ye better than the fowls? And which of you with taking thought can add to his stature one cubit? If ye then be not able to do that thing which is least, why take ye thought for the rest? Consider the lilies how they grow: they toil not, they spin not; and yet I say unto you, that Solomon in all his glory was not arrayed like one of these. If then God so clothe the grass, which is to day in the field, and tomorrow is cast into the oven; how much more will He clothe you, O ye of little faith? And seek not ye what ye shall eat, or what ye shall drink, neither be ye of doubtful mind. For all these things do the nations of the world seek after: and your Father knoweth that ye have need of these things. But rather seek ye* ***the kingdom of God;*** *and all these things shall be added unto you.* (Lu. 12:22-31)

God has shown that if man is to keep **life in the Spirit,** once God imparts that life to him, then he must be content with <u>the true bread!</u> That is, <u>he must hear God's voice and not another's.</u> He must be taught <u>by the Spirit of God only,</u> not by the devil, not by the woman or by man! This is what it means to <u>walk by faith!</u> This, of course, would require one to put all their trust in God instead of themselves! This is what it means to **seek ye the Kingdom of God!**

> *They said therefore unto Him, What sign showest thou then, that we may see, and believe thee? What dost thou work?* ***Our fathers did eat manna in the desert;*** *as it is written,* ***He gave them bread from heaven to eat.*** *The Jesus said unto them, Verily, verily, I say unto you, Moses gave you not that bread from heaven; but my father giveth you* ***the true bread from heaven.*** *For* ***the bread of God is He*** *which cometh down from heaven, and giveth* **life** *unto the world. Then said they unto him, Lord, evermore give us this bread. And Jesus said unto them,* ***I am the bread of Life:*** *He that cometh to me shall never hunger; and he that believeth on me shall never thirst.* (Jo.6:30-35)

The purpose of God from the beginning was to prove what was in the heart of man, whether he would keep His commandments or no, and to teach man that he does not live by bread alone but by every word that proceeds out of the mouth of the Lord! Further, until he was changed (resurrected), in order for the shame of his nakedness not to be revealed, he must be clothed in <u>the righteousness of God</u> **which is by the obedience of faith!**

Now that the Father God had sent Jesus, His only begotten Son, into the world to redeem man from sin and death, it was important that man understand, not only **how to receive life**, but also **how to keep it,** i.e. **inherit eternal life!** God had used the example of the first man Adam to show how through unbelief, life was lost! He then used the example of the Jew (Abraham's natural posterity) that once the life was lost that <u>it could not be regained by the scriptures</u> (i.e. the letter of the Word)! Therefore, Jesus in speaking to the Jews said...

> *And the Father himself, which hath sent me, hath borne witness of me. Ye have neither **heard his voice at any time** nor seen his shape. And ye have not his word abiding in you: for whom he hath sent, **him ye believe not. Search the scriptures;** for in them ye think ye have **eternal life;** and they are they which testify of me. **And ye will not come to me, that ye might have life.*** (Jo. 5:37-40)

Jesus was making it plain that He Himself was <u>the Way, the Truth, and the Life!</u> Life was not something that could be given apart from Himself. It <u>was not </u>a matter of **receiving life from Him.** Rather, if they were to have life, they would have <u>to give themselves to Him,</u> that is, to come under His authority! For He was there as the Shepherd and as the door of the sheepfold.

> *I am the door: by me if any man enter in, he shall be saved, and shall go in and out, and find pasture. The thief cometh not, but for to steal, and to kill, and to destroy: **I am come that they might have life,** and that they might have it more abundantly. I am **the good shepherd:** the good shepherd giveth his life for his sheep. But he*

*that is an hireling, and not the shepherd, whose own the sheep are not, seeth the wolf coming, and leaveth the sheep, and fleeth: and the wolf catcheth them, and scattereth the sheep. The hireling fleeth, because he is an hireling, and careth not for the sheep. **I am the good shepherd, and know my sheep, and am known of mine.** As the Father knoweth me, even so know I the Father: and **I lay down my life for the sheep.** And other sheep I have, which are not of this fold: them also I must bring, and **they shall hear my voice; and there shall be one fold, and one shepherd.** (Jo. 10:9-16)*

When the time came for Jesus <u>to lay down His life for the sheep,</u> He gathered them and said...

*But now I go my way to him that sent me; and none of you asketh me, Wither goest thou? But because I have said these things unto you, sorrow hath filled your heart. Nevertheless I tell you the truth; it is expedient for you that I go away: for if I go not away, **the Comforter will not come unto you;** but if I depart, **I will send him unto you.** And when he is come, he will reprove the world of sin, and of righteousness, and of judgment:* (Jo. 16:5-8)

Until Jesus laid down His life as a ransom for the sheep, there could be no reconciliation back to God. As long as Jesus was in the world as the Good Shepherd, though the Spirit of God was in Him, the Spirit of God was not in the sheep! Jesus knew that until He had fulfilled all that was written of Christ, was crucified, and on the third day was raised again and ascended back to the Father, **the Holy Spirit, the Comforter,** could not be sent. Until **the Spirit of God** could be sent, <u>all were in the flesh!</u> As long as man is in the flesh and not in the Spirit, <u>he is dead in trespasses and sin</u> and <u>cannot walk by faith!</u> By the example of Noah, God had shown from the beginning that salvation was **by faith!** *For whatsoever is not of faith is sin* (Ro. 14:23), *and the wages of sin is death!* (Ro. 6:23) Thus, the scripture teach us...

> *But without faith it is impossible to please Him: for he that cometh to God must believe that he is, and that he is a rewarder of them that diligently seek him.* (He. 11:6)

After Jesus had been offered up for the sins of the world and was risen from the dead, He appeared unto his disciples.

> *To whom also he showed himself alive after his passion by many infallible proofs, being seen of them forty days, and speaking of the things pertaining to **the Kingdom of God**: And, being assembled together with them, commanded them that they should not depart from Jerusalem, but wait for the promise of the Father, which, saith he, ye have heard of me. For John truly baptized with water; but ye shall be baptized with **the Holy Ghost** not many days hence.* (Acts 1:3-5)

It was necessary that the disciples wait for the Holy Ghost (the Comforter and Counselor) to be sent before they made any efforts to be His witnesses. For though they had been baptized by John into the baptism of repentance, they still lacked <u>the power of the Holy Spirit</u>. This alone <u>would restore their soul from death</u> and enable them to walk in <u>the paths of righteousness</u> for His name's sake. (Ps. 23:3) Therefore Jesus told them...

> *But ye shall receive power, after that the Holy Ghost is come upon you: and ye shall be witnesses unto me both in Jerusalem, and in all Judea, and in Samaria, and unto the uttermost part of the earth.* (Acts. 1:8)

Once Jesus finished the work of redemption that the Father had sent Him to do in the world, the way was now open for man to be saved out of the death into which the first Adam had gotten all of mankind. Once <u>saved out of death</u>, man would need to be <u>saved from death</u> (as long as he was still **flesh and blood**) until the final victory over death could be realized. As we have seen, the final victory over death is not realized until <u>resurrection</u>!

> *Now this I say, brethren, that **flesh and blood cannot inherit the kingdom of God;** neither doth corruption **inherit incorruption**. Behold, I show you a mystery: We shall not all sleep, but we shall all be changed, In a moment, in the twinkling of an eye, at the last trump: for the trumpet shall sound, and the dead shall be raised incorruptible, and we shall be changed. For this corruptible must put on incorruption, and this mortal must put on immortality. So when this corruptible shall have put on incorruption, and this mortal shall have put on immortality, then shall be brought to pass the saying that is written: **Death is swallowed up in victory**.* (1Co. 15:50-54)

> *But they which shall be accounted worthy to obtain that world, and **the resurrection from the dead,** neither marry, nor given in marriage: **Neither can they die any more:** for they are*

equal unto angels, and are the children of God, being **the children of the resurrection.** (Lu. 20:35, 36)

In order for us to be saved <u>from death</u>, we must have to be saved from what causes death, until death is swallowed up in victory! In Ro. 8:12, 13 we read what causes death and what is essential to keeping life unto life everlasting.

Therefore, brethren, we are debtors, not to the flesh, to live after the flesh.

For if ye **live after the flesh, ye shall die***; but if ye through the Spirit do mortify the deeds of the body,* **ye shall live.**

As God has shown from the beginning, **life,** once received, could only be kept <u>by obedience to His voice!</u> To live and not die, one must **live after the Spirit, not after the flesh!** However, it is not possible to live after the Spirit until and unless God breathes <u>the breath of life into us</u>. Thus, when the day of Pentecost was fully come, one hundred and twenty disciples were gathered in one accord and in one place.

And suddenly there came a sound from heaven as of a rushing mighty wind, and it filled the entire house where they were sitting. And there appeared unto them cloven tongues like as of fire, and it sat upon each of them. ***And they were all filled with the Holy Ghost,*** *and began to speak with other tongues, as the Spirit gave them utterance.* (Acts 2:2-4)

True to His word, Jesus sent the Holy Spirit to quicken the disciples, to enable them <u>to live after the Spirit,</u> and to go on to perfection! Peter, when explaining to the crowd of Jews who were gathered and amazed at what was happening, said...

> *Therefore let all the house of Israel know assur-edly, that God hath made that **same Jesus,** whom ye have crucified, **both Lord and Christ.** Now when they heard this, they were pricked in their heart, and said unto Peter and to the rest of the apostles, Men and brethren, what shall we do? Then Peter said unto them: **Repent, and be bap-tized every one of you in the name of Jesus Christ for the remission of sins, and ye shall receive the gift of the Holy Ghost.** For the prom-ise is unto you, and to your children, and to all that are afar off, even as many as the Lord our God shall call. And with many other words did he testify and exhort, saying: Save yourselves from this untoward generation.* (Acts 2:36-40)

At last God, through Jesus, had made a provision for mankind to be brought back into <u>the Spirit and Life of God.</u> The way was now open for man who had been sold under sin to come out from under the yoke of sin and the prison house of death and **to walk in the lib-erty and newness of life!** For the yoke of sin could now be broken by <u>the power of the Holy Spirit!</u> All that God required was for man to acknowledge the error of his own way **by repenting** (turning from it) and being baptized for the remission of his sins! The gospel (good news) could now be preached to all men.

> *To wit, that God was in Christ, reconciling the world unto himself, not imputing their trespasses unto them; and hath committed unto us the word of reconciliation. Now then we are ambassadors for Christ, as though God did beseech you by*

us: We pray for you in Christ's stead, be ye rec-
onciled to God. For he hath made him to be sin
*for us, who knew no sin, **that we might be made***
the righteousness of God in him. (2Co. 5:19-21)

The way was now open, and the provision was now
available for man to have <u>his soul delivered out of death</u>
and have <u>his steps ordered by God!</u>

Through the tender mercy of our God; whereby
the dayspring from on high *hath visited us, To*
*give **light** to them that sit in darkness and in the*
*shadow of death, **to guide our feet into the way***
of peace. (Lu. 1:78-79)

*For thou hast **delivered my soul from death:***
*wilt not thou **deliver my feet from falling,** that **I***
may walk before God in the light of the liv-
ing? (Ps. 56:13)

As God forgives us of our sins, quickens us out of
death (restores our soul), and **then leads us by His
Spirit,** we can walk before Him in **the light (life) of the
living.** Only as <u>we walk in the light</u> as <u>He is in the light</u>
can we have unbroken fellowship with the Father and
with his Son, Jesus Christ. Only as we stay in unbroken
fellowship can we know the cleansing power of the
blood!

This then is the message which we have heard
*of him, and declare unto you, **that God is light,***
and in him is no darkness at all. *If we say that*
we have fellowship with him, and walk in dark-
*ness, we lie, and do not the truth: But if **walk in***
***the light**, **as he is in the light,** we have fellow-*
*ship one with another, and **the blood of Jesus***
Christ his Son cleanseth us from all sin. (I Jo.
1:5-7)

Jesus taught when He was here that no man could come unto Him unless the Father, who had sent Him, <u>draw him</u>. It takes a mighty drawing by God for one to overcome the lust of their own flesh and to deliver themselves into the hand of Jesus! Because the lust of one's flesh is also a mighty strong power itself, it will, unless denied, draw one back into his own ways, which are the ways of death! However, for those who are so drawn by God to Jesus (i.e. love the Lord) and who continue in unbroken fellowship with Him, Jesus has promised that He would raise them at the last day (i.e. at the resurrection Jo. 11:24).

> *No man can come to me, except the Father which hath sent me **draw him: and I will raise him up at the last day.** It is written in the prophets, And they shall be all taught of God. Every man therefore that hath heard, and hath learned of the Father, cometh unto me.* (Jo. 6:44, 45)

Anytime we come to the Lord to be saved, it is because the Spirit of God is drawing us. We do not first choose Him, but He chooses us, and for a specific reason.

> *You have not chosen me, but I have chosen you, and ordained you, **that ye should go and bring forth fruit, and that your fruit should remain:** that whatsoever ye shall ask of the Father in my name, he may give it you.* (Jo. 15:16)

The fruit spoken of in the above scripture is the by-product of an unbroken fellowship with the Father and His Son Jesus Christ. As we have seen, it is only as one **lives after the Spirit** that he can have unbroken fellowship with God and bring forth <u>fruit unto holiness</u>.

> *I speak after the manner of men because of the*

*infirmity of your flesh: for as ye have yielded your members servants to uncleanness and to iniquity unto iniquity; even so now yield your members servants to righteousness **unto holiness.** For when ye were the servants of sin, ye were free from righteousness. **What fruit** had ye then in those things whereof ye are now ashamed? For the end of those things is death. **But now being made free from sin,** and **become servants to God, ye have your fruit unto holiness, and the end everlasting life.** For the wages of sin is death; but **the gift of God is eternal life** through Jesus Christ our Lord.* (Ro. 6:19-23)

The above scripture makes clear that <u>eternal life</u> is the reward of bearing fruit unto holiness, and it comes not at the beginning, but at the end of fruit bearing.

As we have seen, God uses trees to represent the kind of lives that we can live. If we live after **the flesh,** <u>we bring forth fruit unto death!</u> If we live after **the letter of God's word** and not **after the Spirit,** we end with <u>withered leaves and no fruit!</u> If we live after **the Spirit**, we will bring forth <u>fruit unto holiness and will receive (inherit) at the end, eternal life!</u> Therefore, Jesus taught...

*Ye shall know them by their fruits. Do men gather grapes of thorns, or figs of thistles? Even so **every good tree bringeth forth good fruit;** but a corrupt tree bringeth forth evil fruit. **A good tree cannot bring forth evil fruit;** neither can a corrupt tree bring forth good fruit. **Every tree that bringeth not forth good fruit is hewn down,** and cast into the fire. **Wherefore by their fruits ye shall know them.** Not every one that saith unto me, Lord, Lord, shall enter into the*

*kingdom of heaven; but **he that doeth the will**
of my father which is in heaven.* (Mt. 7:16-21)

If then we are going to lay hold of (inherit) eternal
life, we must do so by the only way that God has made
such possible. It will not be by just calling Him Lord
but <u>by doing His will!</u> If we are going to bear <u>good
fruit</u>, we must abide in Him, for apart from Him we can
do nothing.

> *I am the true vine, and my Father is the hus-
> bandman. Every branch in me that beareth not
> fruit he taketh away; and every branch that
> beareth fruit he purgeth it, that it may bring forth
> more fruit. **Now ye are clean through the word
> which I have spoken unto you.** Abide in me,
> and I in you. As the branch cannot bear fruit of
> itself, except it abide in the vine; no more can
> ye, except ye abide in me. I am the vine, ye are
> the branches: **He that abideth in me, and I in
> him, the same bringeth forth much fruit:** for
> without me ye can do nothing.* (Jo.15:1-5)

Once we have repented and have been baptized for
the forgiveness of sins, we are clean. All our sins and
transgressions are forgiven. Now we are ready to receive the gift of the Holy Spirit, for only as we are em-
powered and led by the Spirit can we <u>walk in newness
of life!</u> Only as we do what the Spirit teaches us can we
keep His commandments and abide in Him! Only as we
abide in Him can we bear <u>good fruit,</u> be properly clothed
in <u>His righteousness,</u> and not be ashamed before Him at
His coming!

> *But the anointing which ye have received of him
> abideth in you, and ye need not that any man
> teacheth you: but as the same anointing teacheth*

*you of all things, and **is truth,** and is no lie, and
even as **it hath taught you, ye shall abide in
him.** And now, little children, **abide in him;** that,
when he shall appear, we may have confidence,
and **not be ashamed before him at his coming.***
(1Jo. 2:27-28)

As we through obedience to the Spirit abide in Him,
we are able to be partakers of <u>His Life</u>, which is eternal,
for Jesus has already inherited eternal Life by resurrection! Therefore, it is <u>now His life.</u> Thus, He could speak
to John in Re. 1:18 and say, ***I am he that liveth,*** *and was
dead, and, behold, **I am alive forever more,** Amen; and
have the keys of hell and of death.* This is why we are
now saved <u>by His Life</u>! It is living in the way of <u>His
Life</u> that keeps us dead to sin, alive unto God, and walking in the way of His righteousness! This abiding in
Him enables us to now have a foretaste of eternal life
before it becomes our life by inheritance. It is important
for us to understand that God has not given eternal life
to us yet, that is, the life is not **in us,** but only in **His
Son!**

*He that believeth on the Son of God hath the
witness in himself: he that believeth not God hath
made him a liar; because he believeth not the
record that God gave of his Son. And this is the
record that God hath given to us **eternal life,**
and **this life is in his Son.** He that **hath the Son
hath life**; and he that hath not the Son of God
hath not life.*

*These things have I written unto you that be-
lieve on the name of the Son of God; that ye
may know that ye have eternal life, and that ye
may believe on the name of the Son of God.* (1Jo.
5:10-13)

What God does at the time we are initially saved is bring us out of Adam **where we are dead in sin** and then raise us up in Christ **where we are made alive** (1Co.15:22). Thus, we are delivered from so great a death! Once we are saved out of death, we then need to be kept by the power of God from going back into death, until death, our last enemy, is finally overcome by the resurrection! To be so kept, we must keep our trust in God.

*But we had the sentence of death in ourselves that we **should not trust in ourselves, but in God which raiseth the dead:***

***Who delivered** us from so great a death, **and doth deliver**: in whom we trust that he will yet deliver us;* (2Co. 1:9-10)

In the above scripture, we can see the three fold steps, that are involved in getting the victory over death! That is, in laying hold of eternal life! The final act of deliverance from death is by resurrection. This is when mortality is swallowed up of life (2Co. 5:4), and we have been changed! This when we will be born of God and will **inherit eternal life!** Only then will eternal life be our life. Only then will we be no longer subject to death but eternally saved! Not only alive but alive forever more!

*If a man abide not in me, he is cast forth as a branch, and **is withered**; and men gather them, and cast them into the fire, and they are burned.* (Jo. 15:6)

Jesus taught clearly that in order to not become a castaway one must abide in Him. Of course, it is not possible for one to take up *abiding in Him* as long as they are dead in trespasses and sins! So, as we have seen, the first thing that has to happen is for God to save us <u>out of death.</u> This initial step of being saved out of death is <u>all an act of grace</u> on the part of Father God.

> *But God, who is rich in mercy, for his great love wherewith he loved us, Even when we were dead in sins, hath quickened us together with Christ, (by grace ye are saved;)* (Ep. 2:4-5)

This quickening delivers our soul out of death and is accomplished by God's sending His Spirit into our heart. This in turn causes a spiritual awakening to take place (Ga. 4:6, Ro. 8:16) and is referred to as **being born again**. This also raises us up out of the flesh into which man fell and bring us back into the Spirit!

> *Being born again, not of corruptible seed, but of incorruptible, by the word of God, which liveth and abideth for ever.*
>
> *For all flesh is as grass, and all the glory of man as the flower of grass. The grass withereth, and the flower thereof falleth away:*
>
> *But the word of the Lord endureth for ever. And this is the word which by the gospel is preached unto you.* (1Pe. 1:23-25)
>
> *But ye are not in the flesh, but in the Spirit, if so be that the Spirit of God dwell in you. Now if any man have not the Spirit of Christ, he is none of his.*
>
> *And if Christ be in you, the body is dead because of sin; but the Spirit is life because of righteousness.*
>
> *But if the Spirit of him that raised up Jesus from the dead dwell in you, he that raised up Christ from the dead shall also quicken your mortal bodies by his Spirit that dwelleth in you.*

Therefore, brethren, we are debtors, not to the flesh, to live after the flesh.

For if ye live after the flesh, ye shall die: but if ye through the Spirit do mortify the deeds of the body, ye shall live. (Ro. 8:9-13)

We can see by the above scripture that though a born again experience quickens us out of death; it does not remove the possibility of death! Just as Adam before us was subject to death after God had breathed into him the breath of life, and just as Jesus also was subject to death, though He was filled with **the fullness of the Spirit**, <u>so are we,</u> until death is swallowed up in victory by resurrection! The reason this is so, is because we are still corruptible; only our state has changed, <u>not our nature</u>. We can still walk after the flesh and sin, and <u>sin is the sting of death</u> (1Co. 15:56)! Thus, the scriptures teach us that the last enemy to be destroyed is death (1Co. 15:26). This is also why the scriptures teach us that there is a <u>second death</u>. For, if after we have been saved out of the death in which we are in Adam, we are again found in death; we are now twice dead! This time, how-ever, it will not be because of Adam's sin, but our own!

Woe unto them! For they have gone in the way of Cain, and ran greedily after the error of Balaam for reward, and perished in the gain-saying of Core.

*These are spots in your feasts of charity, when they feast with you, feeding themselves **without fear**: clouds they are without water, carried about of winds; **trees whose fruit withereth**, without fruit, **twice dead, plucked up by the roots;***

Raging waves of the sea, foaming out their own

shame; wandering stars, to whom is reserved **the blackness of darkness for ever.** (Jude 1:11-13)

This is the <u>second death</u> out of which there is no recovery! Therefore, no one will ever find themselves in this death because of someone else's sin, <u>but only because of their own!</u>

And I saw a great white throne, and him that sat on it, from whose face the earth and the heaven fled away; and there was found no place for them.

And I saw the dead, small and great, stand before God; and the books were opened: and another book was opened, which is the book of life: and the dead were judged out of those things which were written in the books, **according to their works.**

And the sea gave up the dead which were in it; and death and hell delivered up the dead which were in them: and **they were judged every man according to their works.**

And death and hell were cast into the lake of fire. **This is the second death.**

And whosoever was not found written in the book of life was cast into the lake of fire. (Rev. 20:11-15)

Thus, we can see that God has, from the beginning, been endeavouring to teach us of our need not only to begin in the Spirit, but also to keep ourselves under the covering of His Spirit until mortality has been swallowed up of life! For it is only as we do what the Spirit teaches us that we will not do what the flesh teaches us. It is only as we stay out of the way of the flesh that we can live, continue with the Lord in unbroken fellowship, go up on to perfection (i.e. resurrection), and <u>inherit eternal life!</u> God, in His long suffering for over almost 6,000 years, has now wonderfully shown us that the flesh profits nothing! It is the Spirit that gives life!

> *Be not deceived; God is not mocked: for whatsoever a man soweth, that shall he also reap. For he that soweth to his flesh shall of the flesh reap corruption;* **but he that soweth to the Spirit shall of the Spirit reap life everlasting.** (Ga. 6:7-8)

Anyone who experiences the first step of deliverance out of death (initial salvation) does so because they have found grace in the sight of the God. It is not because of <u>any works of righteousness which they have done.</u> The Jews thought that they had eternal life coming to them because they lived according to the right word. They had drawn back at Mount Sinai from hearing God's voice for fear of loosing <u>their lives</u>. Therefore, they remained ignorant of God's righteousness and gave themselves to establish their own righteousness by the works of the law. In other words, <u>they trusted in themselves</u> that they were able to be righteous by their own works. As we have noted, God, allowed them to embrace this example of error (unbelief), that He might show the way of circumcision in the flesh profits nothing. Since God had already shown by the example of the Gentiles that uncircumcision did not profit, it could now be seen <u>that salvation was impossible apart from God</u>. Though man was responsible for this condition, **he had no ability to recover himself out of it!**

If there was to be a recovery and a going on to perfection for man, God would have to be the One to find the means to do it! God, of course, had already worked out the means by which He would do it before Adam fell, since all the works were finished before the foundation of the world for the recovery of man from the fall (He. 4:3). Since, when man fell from his steadfastness with God, he came under the power of death, he was now helpless and without strength to recover himself. For in his dead state he was separated from God and could not do anything to please God or to merit His favor. Therefore, if there was to be a recovery, it would have to be by **the grace and mercy of God!**

> *But after that the kindness and love of God our Saviour toward man appeared,*
>
> *Not by works of righteousness which we have done, **but according to his mercy he saved us, by the washing of regeneration, and renewing of the Holy Ghost;***
>
> *Which he shed on us abundantly through Jesus Christ our Saviour;*
>
> *That being **justified by his grace**, we should be **made heirs according to the hope of eternal life.*** (Ti. 3:4-7)

There are several things here that we need to see and understand if we are to rightly divide the word of truth. The first is that this initial act of God's saving us is all on the basis of His mercy and grace alone. It comes to us purely as a gift! It is not based on any works of righteousness which we have done. It is totally unmerited on our part. It has to be on this wise, as it is not possible for us to do any works of righteousness apart from Him. This is God first loving us and doing for us what only He can do, that is, forgiving us of all trespasses, purging our conscience from the guilt of sin, releasing us from <u>the penalty of sin,</u> (death), and reconciling us unto Himself. All of this is freely done for us by God in order to enable us to escape the corruption that is in the world through lust and to become partakers of the Divine Nature (II Pe. 1:4), which is love.

Therefore, it is of the utmost importance that, having received forgiveness of sins and having been cleansed by the blood of Jesus, we now walk in obedience to the truth through the Spirit. This is the whole purpose of God in cleansing and quickening us, in bringing us out of death and <u>into His life!</u>

*Therefore we are buried with him by baptism into death: that like as Christ was raised up from the dead by the glory of the Father, even so we also should **walk in newness of life.*** (Ro. 6:4)

This experience of God bringing us out of death into <u>newness of life</u> is <u>our initial experience of salvation.</u> This initial experience happens when one responds to the word of truth by believing the gospel (good news) of our salvation. When one so believes, it is his first time of putting trust in the living God. Until one so responds by repenting and being baptized for the forgiveness of his sins, he is still trusting in himself, that he can find his own way into perfection. This trusting in one's self is called humanism, which is the worshiping of the creature, rather than the Creator! This creature worship is <u>iniquity</u> and is what God took four thousand years to show the end of, that it is not in man to know the way he should go! How then can man direct his own steps? As long as man trusts in man, the way of God is corrupted in the earth, which results in the earth being filled with violence, not peace! This condition in turn brings God's wrath and curse upon man and

the whole earth, as it did in the days of Noah! Indeed,
this rebellion against God and His way is the cause of
the condition of the earth today. *As it was in the days if
Noah, so shall it be also in the days of the Son of man.*
(Lu. 17:26)

If, like Noah, we are going to escape the wrath of
God that is soon coming and the curse that is upon all
flesh that has corrupted His way, then we have to get
out of the ways of the flesh! The only way this escape
is possible, is the way Noah did it—by grace through
faith! The good news is that this way is now open for
all who believe, for all who repent of trusting in themselves and instead, put their trust in the living God and
in His Son, Jesus Christ! When they do this and are
baptized into water for the remission of sins, God freely
forgives all their sins. This forgiveness, in turn, purges
their conscience from dead works and brings them out
from under **the guilt of sin.** It is the shed blood of Jesus
that enables God to lawfully forgive sins, for as God
had shown under the law, with the shedding of blood
there could be forgiveness of sins! This is God justify-
ing us by the blood, i.e. bringing us back to a state of
innocence, just as if we had never sinned!

> But God commendeth his love toward us, in that,
> while we were yet sinners, Christ died for us.
> Much more then, being now **justified by his
> blood,** we shall be saved from **wrath** through
> him. For if, when we were enemies, we were
> reconciled to God by the death of his Son, much
> more, being reconciled, **we shall be saved by
> his life.** (Ro. 5:8-10)

Once we have received forgiveness and cleansing
from all sin, God then breathes **the breath of life** into

us, i.e. quickens us by His Spirit. This brings us out from under **the penalty of sin** and raises us up <u>to walk in newness of Life!</u>

> *Therefore we are buried with him by baptism into death: that like as Christ was raised up from the dead by the glory of the Father, even so we also should* **walk in newness of life.** (Ro. 6:4)

At this time we are delivered out of the body of death and are baptized into the Body of Christ. This deliverance is accomplished by the Spirit of God.

> *For as the body is one, and hath many members, and all the members of that one body, being many, are one body: so also is Christ: For* **by one Spirit we are all baptized into one body,** *whether we be Jews or Gentiles, whether we be bond or free; and* **have been all made to drink into one Spirit.** (I Co. 12:12,13)

This removes us out of the body of sin, the old man (Adam), where we are the servants of sin, and places us in the body of Christ, **the new man,** in which we now become the servants of God (i.e. righteousness).

> *Knowing this, that* **our old man is crucified** *with him, that* **the body of sin** *might be destroyed, that henceforth we* **should not serve sin.** (Ro. 6:6)

This releases us from the captivity to sin and death, into which we are held as long as we are in Adam, and brings us into **the liberty and life of the Spirit in Christ!** Now, as long as we walk after the Spirit (do what the Spirit teaches us), we will <u>abide in Christ</u> and be free from **the law of sin and death!**

> *There is therefore now no condemnation to them* **which are in Christ Jesus,** *who walk not after*

*the flesh, but after the Spirit. For **the law of the
Spirit of life in Christ Jesus** hath made me free
from **the law of sin and death.** For what the
law could not do, in that it was weak through
the flesh, God sending his own Son in the likeness of sinful flesh, and for sin, condemned sin
in the flesh: That the righteousness of the law
might be fulfilled in us, who walk not after the
flesh, but **after the Spirit.** (Ro. 8:1-4)*

As we have noted, it was the plan of God that there
would first be a falling away before **the day of Christ**
would come (II Th. 2:1-3). This falling away was to allow
the man of sin to be revealed before the man of righteousness. If evil was to have its day, it would have to
have its day first, before God ushered in **everlasting
righteousness** (See Dan. 9:24 & II Pe. 3:13). This was to
give man time to discover the unprofitableness of living after the flesh and to repent before God would bring
in **everlasting judgement** (He. 6:2 & Re. 20:11-15)! **In
Adam,** all would experience life after the flesh, the man
of sin. **In Christ** all can experience life after the Spirit,
the man of righteousness. In the first, we are alienated
from the life of God and in darkness; in the second, we
are living in the life of God and in the light! If, when
we are given an opportunity to live in the light we
choose, instead, to live in darkness, it is because we
love darkness, and our deeds are evil.

*And this is the condemnation, that light is come
into the world, and men loved darkness rather
than light, because their deeds were evil. For
every one that doeth evil hateth light, neither
cometh to the light, lest his deeds should be re-
proved. But he that doeth truth cometh to the*

light, that his deeds may be made manifest, that they are wrought in God. (Jo. 3:19-21)

We have seen from the beginning how, given the choice between light and darkness, man has always chosen (loved) the way of darkness (his own way), rather than the way of light (God's way)! Man has believed, that is, he has trusted in himself, that by his own ways (wisdom) and his own works (strength) he can come to perfection, thus, perpetuating himself under **the wrath and curse of God.**

> *Thus saith the* LORD; ***Cursed be the man*** *that trusteth in man, and maketh flesh his arm, and whose heart departeth from the* LORD. *For he shall be like the heath in the desert and shall not see when good cometh; but shall inhabit the parched places in the wilderness, in a salt land not inhabited.*

> ***Blessed is the man*** *that trusteth in the* LORD, *and whose hope the* LORD *is. For he shall be as a tree planted by the waters, and that spreadeth out her roots by the river, and shall not see when heat cometh, but her leaf shall be green; and shall not be careful in the year of drought, neither shall cease from yielding fruit. The heart is deceitful above all things, and desperately wicked: who can know it?* ***I the*** LORD ***search the heart, I try the reins, even to give every man according to his own ways, and according to the fruit of his own doings.*** (Je. 17:5-10)

As we have seen, the initial act of God's bringing us out of death in Adam and into life in Christ is all based on God's love, mercy, and grace. It is not based on any works of righteousness we have done, for apart from

Him we can do none! However, when God in His love draws us to Jesus, washes us clean by His blood, in His mercy forgives us of all our sins, and then by His grace quickens us out of death, it is all for bringing us out from being servants to sin and into being servants of righteousness. After <u>being made free from sin</u> and being no longer defiled by sin, we can now be joined (married) to Him!

> *Wherefore, my brethren, ye are also become dead to the law by the body of Christ; that **ye should be married to another,** even to Him who is raised from the dead, that we should bring forth fruit unto God.* (Ro. 7:4)

Only after we have been so joined (married) to Him can He search out what is now in our hearts, whether we will obey His voice or not! Then begins the trial of our faith and the test of our love toward Him. For the only way we can stay joined to Him is to obey His voice, i.e. keep His commandments, which we will only do if we love Him more than we love ourselves! It is only by staying so joined to Him that He can lead us in the right way and bring us into the reward of the inheritance! Only He knows the way that will bring us to perfection, where we will not only be alive, but we will be alive forevermore; where death is swallowed up in victory, **where, we will not only be saved, but also eternally saved!** Thus, the scriptures teach us that obedience is better than sacrifice (I Sa. 15:22). By the sacrifice of Christ (His death) we can be reconciled to God, but only by **His life** can we be saved! To be reconciled to God only requires us to receive Jesus, but to be eternally saved requires us to **obey Him!** *And being made perfect, He became the author of **eternal salvation** unto all who*

obey Him. (He. 5:9). In laying down His life for the sheep, Jesus showed His love for the Father and the sheep. In laying down our life in order to live in His life we, as the sheep, show our love for Him and one another. The reason we are put to this test of love is because all that God has prepared in the way of an inheritance, He prepared it for those that love Him, as shown in I Co. 2:9. *But as it is written, Eye hath not seen, nor ear heard, neither have entered into the heart of man, the things which God hath prepared* **for them that love Him.** In Ja. 1:12 we read: *Blessed is the man that endureth temptation: for when he is tried, he shall receive* **the crown of life,** *which the Lord hath promised* **to them that love Him.**

And because iniquity shall abound, the love of many shall wax cold. **But he that shall endure unto the end, the same shall be saved.** *And this gospel of the kingdom shall be preached in all the world for a witness unto all nations; and then shall the end come.* (Mt. 24:12-14)

Now the God of peace, that brought again from the dead our Lord Jesus, that great shepherd of the sheep, through the blood of the everlasting covenant, Make you perfect in every good work to do his will, working in you that which is well-pleasing in his sight, through Jesus Christ; to whom be glory for ever and ever. Amen. (He. 13:20,21)

Part II
Rapture Or Resurrection

The idea that the church will be raptured out of this world at the end of this age was first introduced into Christian teaching in the latter part of the nineteenth century by a man named Darby. This teaching then gained wide acceptance through the teachings of Dr. C. I. Scofield. This doctrine was not taught by any of the early church fathers; and as a matter of fact, the word **rapture** is not even in the Bible.

The idea of a rapture, however, has a great appeal, for such is to be preferred over the idea of one being able to enter the Kingdom of God only through much tribulation!

The fact that the early apostles of the church understood that it is through much tribulation is clearly seen in Acts 14: 21, 22.

*And when they had preached the gospel to that city, and had taught many, they returned to Lystra, and to Iconium, and Antioch, confirming the souls of the disciples and exhorting them to continue in the faith, and that we **must through much tribulation** enter into the Kingdom of God.*

A popular teaching is that the Gentile church will be raptured out, and that the Jewish remnant will remain here on earth to usher in the one thousand year reign of Christ over the nations. The scripture plainly states, however, that the church is nether Jewish nor Gentile, but that God in Christ has broken down the middle wall of partition, for to make in Himself of the twain one man! He did this that He might reconcile both unto God in **one body** (Ep. 2:14-16)! Therefore, there is not a Gentile church and a Jewish church! There are not two bodies of believers; there is only one! This is plainly seen as well in Ep. 4:4: *There is one body, and one spirit, even as you are called in one hope of your calling.*

In I Co.15:38, the scripture states that unto every seed, is given his own body. There is, therefore, the body of the Gentiles, the body of the Jews, and the body of Christ! It is clear in Ep.1:6 that the only place of acceptance of Jew or Gentile is in Christ! II Co. 5:7 states: *Therefore if any man be in Christ he is a new creature: old things are passed away; behold, all things are become new.* We read in Ga. 3:27, 28:

> *For as many of you as have been baptized into Christ have put on Christ. There is neither Jew nor Greek, there is neither bond nor free, there is neither male nor female: for ye are all one in Christ Jesus.*

Further, we can see by the prayer of Jesus in Jo. 17:15 that it is not God's intention to rapture the church out of the world: *I pray not that thou shouldest take them out of the world but that thou shouldest keep them from the evil.*

The church is sown in corruption (i.e., this world, for as I Jo. 5:19 states: "...the whole world lieth in wickedness.") that it might be **raised** in incorruption (I Co. 15:42). We can see therefore that the way up or out is not

rapture but resurrection! What the church needs to bring
it up into incorruptibility and out of mortality into immortality is not a geographical change from earth to
heaven, but rather a change of what we are! A change
from being mortal, corruptible, earthy, to being immortal, incorruptible, heavenly! That this change takes in
resurrection is clearly taught in I Co. 15:49-54:

> *And as we have born the image of the earthy,*
> *we shall also bear the image of the heavenly.*
> *Now this I say, brethren, that flesh and blood*
> *cannot inherit the kingdom of God; neither doth*
> *corruption inherit incorruption. Behold, I show*
> *you a mystery; we shall not all sleep, but we*
> *shall all be **changed**. In a moment, in the twin-*
> *kling of an eye, at the last trump: for the trum-*
> *pet shall sound, and the dead shall be raised*
> *incorruptible, and we shall be changed. For this*
> *corruptible must put on incorruption, and this*
> *mortal must put on immortality. So when this*
> *corruptible shall have put on incorruption, and*
> *this mortal shall have put on immortality, then*
> *shall be brought to pass the saying that is writ-*
> *ten, Death is swallowed up in victory.*

The last enemy of the church to be destroyed is death
(I Co. 15:26). We can see that it is only by the means of
resurrection that death is overcome! What qualifies one
for the resurrection is clearly taught by Paul in Ph. 3:7-
12:

> *But what things were gain to me, those I counted*
> *loss for Christ. Yea doubtless, and I count all*
> *things but loss for the excellency of the knowl-*
> *edge of Christ Jesus my Lord: for whom I have*
> *suffered the loss of all things, and do count them*

*as dung that I may win Christ, and be found in Him, not having my own righteousness, which is of the law, but that which is through the faith of Christ, the righteousness which is of God by faith: That I may know Him, and **the power of His resurrection,** and the fellowship of His sufferings, being made conformable unto His death; If by any means **I might attain unto the resurrection of the dead.** Not as though I had already attained, either were already **perfect:** but I follow after, if that I may apprehend that for which also I am apprehended of Christ Jesus.*

What is involved in knowing the fellowship of His sufferings is revealed to us in I Pe. 4:1, 2:

FORASMUCH then as Christ has suffered for us in the flesh, arm yourselves likewise with the same mind: for he that hath suffered in the flesh hath ceased from sin: That he no longer should live the rest of his time in the flesh to the lusts of men, but to the will of God.

What is involved in being made conformable unto His death is revealed to us in Ro. 6:10-12:

For in that He died, He died unto sin once: but in that He liveth, He liveth unto God. Likewise reckon ye also yourselves to be dead indeed unto sin, but alive unto God through Jesus Christ our Lord. Let not sin therefore reign in your mortal body, that ye should obey it in the lusts thereof.

Ro. 6:1-5: What shall we say then? Shall we continue in sin, that grace may abound? God forbid. How shall we, that are dead in sin, live any longer therein? Know ye not that so many of us as were baptized into Jesus Christ were bap-

*tized into His death? Therefore, we are buried
with Him by baptism into death: that like as
Christ was raised up from the dead by the glory
of the Father, even so we should walk in newness of life. For if we have been planted together in the likeness of His death, we shall be
also in the likeness of His resurrection.*

Any failure, therefore, to be in the likeness of His
resurrection, has its roots in our failure to be conformed
unto His death, which death is a death **to** sin! In order
for us to escape being dead **in** sin, we must be dead **to**
sin. This death **to** sin is essential to our knowing the
Lord and being found in Him, for in Him there is no
sin (I Jo. 3:5). *Whosoever abideth in Him sinneth not:
Whosoever sinneth hath not seen Him, neither known
Him.* (I Jo. 3:6)

The idea that the church is going to be raptured up
to heaven and perfected there, and then return with
Christ, is not scriptural. God's will and purpose for the
church is revealed in Ep. 1:9, 10:

*Having made known unto us the mystery of His
will, according to His good pleasure which He
has purposed in Himself: That in the dispensa-
tion of the fullness of times He might gather together in one all things in Christ, both which
are in heaven, and which are on earth: even in
Him;*

The reason for this is that being in earth or in heaven
doesn't make one **perfect,** but being in Christ does! We
can see this clearly in Col. 1:27, 28:

*To whom God would make know what is the
riches of the glory of this mystery among the
Gentiles; which is Christ in you, the hope of*

*glory; Whom we preach, warning every man, and teaching every man in all wisdom; that we may present every man **perfect in Christ Jesus:***

*For in Him dwelleth all the fullness of the Godhead bodily. And ye are **complete** in Him, which is the head of all principality and power.* (Col. 2:9, 10)

This is why the apostle Paul said that he wanted to be found in Him (Ph. 3:9). We must be found in Him in order to be presented perfect and attain unto the resurrection of the dead!

Therefore Jesus Himself taught while He was here the importance of our abiding in Him:

I am the vine and ye are the branches. He that abideth in Me, and I in him, the same bringeth forth much fruit: for without Me you can do nothing. If a man abide not in Me, he is cast forth as a branch, and is withered; and men gather them, and cast them into the fire, and they are burned. (Jo. 15:5,6)

The means of abiding in Him is taught in I Jo. 2:27, 28:

But the anointing which ye have received of Him abideth in you, and you need not that any man teach you: but as the same anointing teacheth you of all things, and is truth, and is no lie, and even as it hath taught you, ye shall abide in Him. And now, little children, abide in Him; that when He shall appear, we may have confidence, and not be ashamed before Him at His coming.

If we are to avoid being ashamed at His coming and being disqualified for the **first resurrection,** we must

be found in Him! We read about the **first resurrection**
in Rev. 20:5, 6:

> *But the rest of the dead lived not again until the
> thousand years were finished. This is the **first
> resurrection.** Blessed and holy is he that hath
> part in the **first resurrection:** on such the sec-
> ond death has no power, but they shall be priests
> of God and of Christ, and shall reign with Him
> a thousand years.*

Concerning being found in Him, we read about this
in Philippians 3:9-14:

> *And be found in Him, not having mine own righ-
> teousness, which is of the law, but that which is
> through the faith of Christ, the righteousness
> which is of God by faith: That I may know Him,
> and the power of His resurrection, and the fel-
> lowship of His sufferings, being made conform-
> able unto His death; If by any means I might
> attain unto the resurrection of the dead. Not as
> though I had already attained, either were al-
> ready perfect: but I follow after, if that I may
> apprehend that for which also I am apprehended
> of Christ Jesus. Brethren, I count not myself to
> have apprehended: but this one thing I do, for-
> getting those things which are behind, and
> reaching forth unto those things which are be-
> fore, I press toward the mark for the prize of the
> high calling of God in Christ Jesus.*

The Lord is coming back, not for an imperfect
church, but for a perfect one! Ephesians verifies this in
the following verses, Ep. 5:25-27:

> *Husbands, love your wives, even as Christ also*

loved the church, and gave Himself for it; That
He might sanctify it and cleanse it with the wash-
ing of water by the word. That He might present
it to Himself a glorious church, not having spot,
*or wrinkle, or any such thing; but that **it should***
be holy and without blemish.

This perfection must be realized before He comes
or we will not be ready! We read about this in Matthew
25: 6-13:

And at midnight there was a cry made, Behold,
the Bridegroom cometh; go ye out to meet Him.
Then all those virgins arose, and trimmed their
lamps. And the foolish said unto the wise, Give
us of your oil; for our lamps are gone out. But
the wise answered, saying, Not so; lest there be
not enough for us and you: but go ye rather to
them that sell, and buy for yourselves. And while
they went to buy, the Bridegroom came; and they
that were ready went in with Him to the mar-
riage: and the door was shut. Afterward came
also the other virgins saying, Lord, Lord, open
to us. But He answered and said, Verily I say
unto you, I know you not. Watch therefore, for
ye know neither the day nor the hour wherein
the Son of man cometh.

Clearly the careless and ill prepared will be shut out,
not raptured! That this is true can also be seen in Luke
13:23-28:

Then said one unto Him, Lord, are there few
that be saved? And He said unto them; Strive to
*enter in at **the strait gate:** for many, I say unto*
you, will seek to enter in, and shall not be able.
When once the master of the house is risen up,

*and hath shut to the door, and ye begin to stand
without, and to knock at the door, saying, Lord,
Lord, open unto us; and He shall answer and
say unto you, I know you not whence ye are:
Then shall ye begin to say, We have eaten and
drunk in Thy presence, and Thou hast taught in
our streets: But He shall say, I tell you, I know
not whence ye are; depart from Me, all ye work-
ers of iniquity. There shall be weeping and
gnashing of teeth, when ye shall see Abraham,
and Isaac, and Jacob, and all the prophets, in
the Kingdom of God, and you yourselves are
thrust out.*

Certainly there has been no rapture for all the saints
before us who have fought a good fight, finished their
course, and kept the faith. They do have, however, a
crown of righteousness coming, which the Lord, the
righteousness judge, will give them at that day! These
will not be ashamed at His coming, but will love His
appearing:

*I have fought a good fight, I have finished my
course, I have kept the faith: Henceforth there
is laid up for me a crown of righteousness, which
the Lord, the righteous judge, shall give me at
that day: and not to me only, but unto all them
that love His appearing.* (II Tim. 4:7,8)

The idea that Mt. 24:37-51 speaks of the rapture of the
church is not verified by scripture, for in the teachings
of the rapture the righteous are gathered out and the
wicked are left. The scripture clearly states, however,
that the wicked are gathered out and only the righteous
shall remain, even as it was in the days of Noah!

For as in the days that were before the flood

*they were eating and drinking, marrying and giving in marriage, until the day that Noah entered the ark, and knew not until the flood came, and **took them all away;** so shall also the coming of the Son of man be.* (Mt. 24:38, 39)

The plain teaching of Jesus in Mt. 13:38-51 is that the wicked are gathered out and the righteous remain:

*As therefore the tares are gathered and burned in the fire; so shall it be at the end of this world. The Son of man shall send forth His angels, and they shall gather out of His kingdom all things that offend, and them which do iniquity: And shall cast them into a furnace of fire: there shall be wailing and gnashing of teeth. **Then shall the righteous shine forth as the sun in the Kingdom of their Father.** Who hath ears to hear, let him hear.*

The Old Testament verifies as well that the righteous shall never be removed!

*For the upright shall dwell in the land, and **the perfect shall remain in it.** But the wicked shall be cut off from the earth, and the transgressors shall be rooted out of it.* (Pv. 2:21, 22)

Ps. 104:35 states: *Let the sinners be consumed out of the earth, and let the wicked be no more.*

Is. 13:9 states: *Behold the day of the Lord cometh, cruel both with wrath and fierce anger, to lay the land desolate: and **He shall destroy the sinners out of it.***

This is why the apostle Paul taught the church in Ep. 6:13:

Wherefore take unto you the whole armor of God

> *that you may be able to withstand in the evil day, and having done all, to stand.*

Thus the question in Mal. 3:2 and Rev. 6:17 is not who will be raptured, but who will be able to stand?

> *But who may abide the day of His coming? And who shall stand when He appeareth? For He is like a refiner's fire, and like fullers' soap.* (Mal. 3:2)

> *For the great day of His wrath is come; and who shall be able to stand* (Rev. 6:17)?

Further Hebrews 12:25-29 teaches us that what will be removed is all that can be shaken, and that only those things that cannot be shaken shall remain. In verses 28 and 29 we read:

> *Wherefore we receiving a kingdom which **cannot be moved,** let us have grace, whereby we may serve God acceptably with reverence and godly fear: For our God is a consuming fire.*

Another scripture that is used to support the idea of a rapture is found in I Th. 4:14-17:

> *For if we believe that Jesus **died and rose again,** even so them also which sleep in Jesus will God bring with Him. For this we say unto you by the word of the Lord, that we which are alive and remain unto the coming of the Lord shall not prevent them which are asleep. For the Lord himself shall descend from heaven with a shout, with the voice of the archangel, and with the trump of God: and the dead in Christ shall rise first: Then we which are alive and remain shall be caught up together with them in the clouds, to meet the Lord in the air: and so shall we ever be with the Lord.*

Note in verse 14 that the apostle Paul is pointing out that as Jesus died and rose again, in like manner God will bring forth those which sleep in Jesus (i.e., all who have kept the faith but are not physically alive at the time of this great event). Paul, speaking to the Corinthian church about this same matter, had this to say: *Knowing that He which raised up the Lord Jesus shall raise up us also by Jesus, and shall present us with you* (II Co. 4:14). We also want to note that the saints spoken of here are not being raptured off to heaven. But rather they are those who have died physically and have gone to be with the Lord in heaven, and they are now being brought with Him as He descends from heaven! That this event is speaking of resurrection, not rapture, can be seen by the fact that at the sound of the trump of God, the dead in Christ **rise first!** Paul gives in greater detail a description of this event in I Co. 15: We look again at verses 51, 52:

> *Behold, I shew you a mystery; We shall not all sleep, but we shall all be changed, In a moment, in the twinkling of an eye, at the last trump: For the trumpet shall sound, and the dead (that is the dead in Christ) shall be **raised** incorruptible, and we shall be changed.*

There will be those who have kept the faith and are asleep in Jesus, and there will be those who have kept the faith and are alive and remain unto the time of this great event. Both will be changed in a moment, in the twinkling of an eye, at the sound of the trump! This will complete the perfecting of the saints and will enable them to know both the Lord, and **the power of His resurrection!** It is in **resurrection** that we shall come forth out of death into His likeness! It is in **resurrection** that corruptible puts on incorruption, mortal puts on immortality, and death, the last enemy, is swallowed up in victory! It is only by our coming to know Jesus **and the power of His resurrection** that we will be able to join Him where He is, and fulfil the prayer that He prayed in Jo.17:24: *Father, I will that they also, whom Thou hast given Me, be with me where I am: that they may behold My glory.* In I Co. 15:42, 43 we read:

> *So also is the resurrection of the dead. It is sown in corruption; it is raised in incorruption: It is sown in dishonour; it is raised in glory.*

Jesus said of all who try to climb up some other way:

> *Verily, verily, I say unto you, He that entereth not by the door into the sheepfold, but climbeth up some other way, the same is a thief and a robber.* (Jo. 10: 1)

I Th. 4:16, states:

> *The Lord Himself shall descend from heaven with a shout, with the voice of the archangel, and with the trump of God; and the dead in Christ **shall rise first:** Then we which are alive and remain shall be caught up together with them in the clouds, to meet the Lord in the air: and so shall we ever be with the Lord.*

Scofield notes that this is the setting forth of the return of Christ, the rapture of the church, and the re-union of all believers (see Scofield's notes on I Th. 4:17). However, as we have noted, this is **not** the setting forth of a description of the church being raptured to heaven. The place of meeting the Lord with all the saints is not in heaven, but in the air! The word **air** used here is the same as used in Ep. 2:2, where it tells us that when we walk according to the course of this world, we are walking according to "the prince of the power of the air!" The word **air** here is a description of the realm **the devil** has been given by God to operate in as the god of this world; where, as an angel of light, he blinds men to the truth and deceives the nations, as described in the following verses:

> II Cor. 4:4: *In whom the god of this world hath blinded the minds of them which believe not.*

> Re. 20:3,7,8: *And cast him into the bottomless pit, and shut him up, and set a seal upon him, that he should deceive the nations no more, till the thousand years should be fulfilled: and after he must be loosed a little season. And when the thousand years are expired, Satan shall be loosed from his prison, "And shall go out to deceive the nations which are in the four quarters of the earth, Gog, and Magog, to gather them together to battle: the number of whom is as the sand of the sea.*

Obviously, God uses the devil as "the prince of the power of the air" to serve His purposes. We can see that this is so when we note that as soon as Jesus was baptized by John the Baptist in the River Jordan, He was led by the Spirit of God into the wilderness to be tempted of the devil! *Then was Jesus led up of the Spirit into the wilderness to be tempted of the devil* (Mat. 4:1). We can further see how God uses the devil in II Th. 2:9-11 as the one working

> *...with all deceivableness of unrighteousness in them that perish; because they received not the love of the truth that they might be saved. And for this cause God will send them strong delusion, that they should believe a lie.*

Jesus, speaking about the devil in Jo. 8:44, said:

He was a murderer from the beginning, and abode not in the truth, because there is no truth in him. When he speaketh a lie, he speaketh of his own: for he is a liar and a father of it.

That God has complete control over the devil is clearly seen by the fact that when He no longer has need for the devil to do his work, God puts him away with one angel!

And I saw an angel come down from heaven, having the key of the bottomless pit and a great chain in his hand. And he laid hold on the dragon, the old serpent, which is the devil, and Satan, and bound him a thousand years. (Re. 20:1, 2)

When God has need of him again, He releases him out of his prison:

And when the thousand years are expired, Satan shall be loosed out of his prison. And shall got out to deceive the nations which are in the four quarters of the earth, Gog and Magog, to gather them together in battle: the number of them is as the sand of the sea. (Re. 20:7, 8)

We can see by the above Scriptures how God will then use the devil once again to deceive all the nations that love not the truth (i.e. goat nations, called Gog and Magog) and to gather them together to battle! After this final testing of the nations, God will have no further use of the devil. God will have by then used him first to sift the saints, as can be seen in Luke 22:31, *And the Lord said, Simon, Simon, behold, Satan hath desired to have you, that he may sift you as wheat.* Then as we have seen, God will use him finally to sift the nations, after which he is put away once and for all in the lake of fire!

> *And the devil that deceived them was cast into the lake of fire and brimstone, where the beast and the false prophet are, and shall be tormented day and night for ever and ever.* (Re. 20:10)

We can see, then, that the coming of the Lord and at the time of our being gathered together unto Him (II Th. 2:1) that the place we are going to meet Him is in the air. This is the very place where the devil has had his power as the god of this world, and as the prince of the power of the air! The time of this great event is also spoken of in Daniel 7:13-18:

> *I saw in the night visions, and behold, one like the Son of man came with the clouds of heaven, and came to the Ancient of days, and they brought him near before him. And there was given him dominion, and glory, and a kingdom, that all people, nations, and languages, should serve him: his dominion is an everlasting dominion, which shall not pass away, and his kingdom that which shall not be destroyed . . . But the saints of the most High shall take the kingdom, and possess the kingdom for ever, even for ever and ever.*

> Daniel 7:27: *And the kingdom and dominion, and the greatness of the kingdom under the whole heaven, shall be given to the people of the saints of the most High, whose kingdom is an everlasting kingdom, and all dominions shall serve and obey him.*

We also read about this future event in Re. 11:15:

And the seventh angel sounded; and there were

*great voices in heaven saying, The kingdoms of this world are become **the kingdoms of our Lord and of His Christ**; and He shall reign for ever and ever.*

For as it says in He. 2:5: For unto the angels (i.e. the devil and his angels) hath He not put in subjection the world (age) to come.

The reference in Re. 11:15 to "our Lord and His Christ," is the Holy Spirit pointing out that the reins of the government over the age or world to come will be given to Jesus and His brethren! These are those who have by resurrection come forth unto a perfect man, unto the fullness of the stature of Christ! For all who hold their confidence steadfast unto the end are made **partakers of Christ!** As it says in He. 3:14: *For we are made partakers of Christ, if we hold the beginning of our confidence steadfast unto the end.*

Among these partakers of Christ are those saints that have gone before us and are now asleep in Jesus, spoken of in He. 11:33-35:

> *...Who through faith subdued kingdoms, wrought righteousness, obtained promises, stopped the mouth of lions, quenched the violence of fire, escaped the edge of the sword, out of weakness were made strong, waxed valiant in fight, turned to flight the armies of the aliens. Women received their dead raised to life again: and others were tortured, not accepting deliverance; that they might obtain **a better resurrection.***

Note that all these are not looking forward to a rapture, but rather to **a better resurrection!** They are having to wait, however, for the rest of their brethren, as it says in He. 11:39, 40:

> *And these all, having obtained a good report through faith, received not the promise: God having provided some better thing for us, that they without us should not **be made perfect.***

That this "being made perfect" is accomplished by resurrection, and not by rapture, again is made clear by the apostle Paul in Ph. 3:10-12.

> *That I may know Him, and the power of His resurrection, and the fellowship of His sufferings, being made conformable unto His death; if by any means I might attain unto the resurrection of the dead. Not as though I had already attained, either were **perfect**: but I follow after, if that I may apprehend that for which also I am apprehended of Christ Jesus.*

All who apprehend that for which they have been apprehended of Christ Jesus will not be in a rapture, but in something far better: **A better resurrection!** The better resurrection is the **first resurrection!** We read about this **better resurrection** in Rev. 20:5, 6:

> *But the rest of the dead lived not again until the thousand years were finished. This is the **first resurrection**. Blessed and holy is he that hath part in the **first resurrection**: on such the second death hath no power, but they shall be priests of God and of Christ, and shall reign with Him a thousand years.*

As we have seen, this **first resurrection** is to take place at the coming of our Lord! The resurrection is what perfects us and brings us up out of the realm of the dead into the realm of incorruptibility, immortality and glory, where Jesus is! All who attain unto this **first resurrection** will be ready to rule and reign with Jesus over

the nations, replacing the devil and his angels, who are
present rulers and powers of the darkness! Re. 14:1-4
pictures for us these "first fruits" unto God and to the
Lamb:

> *And I looked, and, lo, a Lamb stood on the mount
> Zion, and with Him an hundred forty and four
> thousand, having His Father's name written in
> their foreheads. And I heard a voice from heaven,
> as the voice of many waters, and as the voice of
> a great thunder: and I heard the voice of harp-
> ers harping with their harps: And they sung as
> it were a new song before the throne, and be-
> fore the four beasts, and the elders: and no man
> can learn that song but the hundred and forty
> four thousand, which were redeemed from the
> earth. These are they which were not defiled with
> women; for they are virgins. These are they
> which follow the Lamb whithersoever He goeth.
> These were redeemed among men, being the **first
> fruits** unto God and to the Lamb.*

In Re. 20:4, we can see that those who have attained
unto the first resurrection will have judgment commit-
ted unto them, and they shall live and reign with Christ
over the nations a thousand years. This is the promise
of the Lord to the church in Re. 2:26, 27:

> *And he that overcometh, and keepeth my works
> unto the end, to him will I give power over the
> nations: And he shall rule with them with a rod
> of iron: as the vessels of a potter shall they be
> broken to shivers: even as I received of my Fa-
> ther.*

And in Re. 3:21: *To him that overcometh will I grant
to sit with Me in My throne. Also* Re. 19:14, 15, we are

given a picture of the Lord's coming with His saints to set up God's kingdom on earth, and to execute judgement over the nations:

> *And the armies which were in heaven followed Him upon white horses, clothed in fine linen, white and clean. And out of His mouth goeth a sharp sword, that with it He should smite the nations: and He shall rule them with a rod of iron: and He treadeth the winepress of the fierceness and wrath of Almighty God.*

As we have seen, at this time the devil will be removed as "the god of this world" and will be shut up in the bottomless pit for the time of the one-thousand-year reign of the Lord and His Christ, during which time he will not be able to deceive the nations as before. Therefore, as it says in Hab. 2:14: *The earth shall be filled with the knowledge of the glory of the Lord as the waters cover the sea.* Also in Is. 11:1-9 we are given a more detailed description of this time:

> *And there shall come forth a rod out of the stem of Jesse, and a Branch shall grow out of his roots: And the spirit of the LORD shall rest upon him, the spirit of wisdom and understanding, the spirit of counsel and might, the spirit of knowledge and of the fear of the LORD; And shall make him of quick understanding in the fear of the LORD: and he shall not judge after the sight of his eyes, neither reprove after the hearing of his ears: But with righteousness shall he judge the poor, and reprove with equity for the meek of the earth: and he shall smite the earth with the rod of his mouth, and with the breath of his lips shall he slay the wicked. And righteousness shall*

*be the girdle of his loins, and faithfulness the
girdle of his reins. The wolf also shall dwell
with the lamb, and the leopard shall lie down
with the kid; and the calf and the young lion
and the fatling together; and a little child shall
lead them. And the cow and the bear shall feed;
their young ones shall lie down together: and
the lion shall eat straw like the ox. And the suck-
ing child shall play on the hole of the asp, and
the weaned child shall put his hand on the cocka-
trice' den. They shall not hurt nor destroy in all
the holy mountain: for the earth shall be full of
the knowledge of the Lord, as the waters cover
the sea.*

This peace and safety on earth, which will be the
result of the kingdoms of this world becoming the kingdoms of our Lord and His Christ is what the whole creation is waiting for:

*For the earnest expectation of the creature
waiteth for **the manifestation of the sons of God.**
For the creature was made subject to vanity, not
willingly, but by reason of him who hath sub-
jected the same in hope, because the creature
itself also shall be delivered from the bondage
of corruption into the glorious liberty of the children of God. For we know that the whole creation groaneth and travaileth in pain together
until now. And not only they, but ourselves also,
which have the firstfruits of the Spirit, even we
ourselves groan within ourselves, waiting for the
adoption, to wit, the redemption of our body* (Ro.
8:19-23).

What then is the earnest expectation of the creation?

Not the rapture of the church, but **the manifestation of
the sons of God!**

We also can see what we, who have the firstfruits of
the Spirit, are waiting for is not a rapture, but the final
act of redemption as sons, which will be the redemption
of our bodies! This is when the Lord will change our
vile body like unto His glorious body (Ph. 3:21)! When
and how will this happen?

> *But some man will say, How are the dead raised
> up? And with what **body** do they come? Thou
> fool, that which thou soweth is not quickened,
> except it die: And that which thou soweth, thou
> soweth not that **body** that shall be, but bare
> grain, it may chance of wheat, or of some other
> grain; But God giveth it a **body** as it hath pleased
> Him, and to every seed his own body.*

> *So also is the resurrection of the dead. It is sown
> in corruption; it is raised in incorruption: It is
> sown in dishonour; it is raised in glory: It is
> sown in weakness; it is raised in power: It is
> sown in **a natural body;** it is raised in **a spiri-
> tual body.** (I Co.15: 35-38, 42 -44)*

Until the sons of God experience the final act of
redemption (i.e. the bodily change that takes place only
in resurrection), it is not yet time for them to be mani-
fested, for it does not yet appear what they shall be:

> *Behold what manner of love the Father has be-
> stowed upon us the we should be called the sons
> of God: Beloved, now are we the sons of God,
> and it doth not yet appear what we shall be.*
> (I Jo. 3:1, 2)

Jo. 1: 12 tells us that as many as receive Him, to them
gave He power (authority) to become the sons of God,

even to them that believe on His name. We read also in He. 2:10 that it is God's purpose to bring many sons to glory:

> *For it became Him, for whom are all things, and by whom are all things, in bringing many sons unto glory, to make the captain of their salvation perfect through sufferings.*

As has been shown, the Scripture clearly teaches that sonship is realized by **resurrection**, not by rapture. It is only by **resurrection,** not rapture, that one can be changed from corruptible to incorruptible, from mortal to immortal, and not be only alive, but alive forever more, as death is swallowed up in victory!

> *So when this corruptible shall have put on incorruption, and this mortal shall have put on immortality, then shall be brought to pass the saying that is written, Death is swallowed up in victory.* (I Co. 15:54)

Having been sown in dishonour, the sons will be raised in glory; having been sown in weakness, they will be raised in power, as is stated in I Co. 15:43: *It is sown in dishonour it is raised in glory: it is sown in weakness; it is raised in power:*

In this way all the sons shall be changed! *Behold I shew you a mystery; We shall not all sleep, but we shall all be changed* (I Cor. 15:51).

Then they shall be just like Him, for this is the purpose in God calling them!

> *For whom He did foreknow, He also did predestinate to be conformed to the image of His son, that He might be the first born among many brethren.* (Ro. 8:29).

When Jesus was questioned by certain Sadducees, that denied that there is a resurrection, they asked Him:

Saying, Master, Moses wrote unto us, If any man's brother die, having a wife, and he die without children, that his brother should take his wife, and raise up seed unto his brother. There were therefore seven brethren: and the first took a wife, and died without children. And the second took her to wife, and he died childless. And the third took her; and in like manner the seven also: and they left no children, and died. Last of all the woman died also. Therefore in the resurrection whose wife of them is she? For seven had her to wife. (Lu. 20:28-33)

In Luke 20:34-36, Jesus answered:

Jesus answering said unto them, the children of this world marry, and are given in marriage, but they which shall be accounted worthy to obtain that world, and the resurrection from the dead, neither marry, nor are given in marriage. Neither can they die anymore: For they are equal unto the angels; and are the children (sons) of God, being the children of the resurrection.

Those who are **accounted worthy** to obtain unto this grand and glorious event will be the "firstfruits" unto God and the Lamb, and ready to be glorified together with Christ:

The Spirit itself beareth witness with our spirit, that we are the children of God: And if children, then heirs; heirs of God, and joint heirs with Christ, if so be that we suffer with Him, that we may be also glorified together. (Rom. 8:16, 17)

Jesus was speaking of this very thing to His disciples in Jo. 6:38-40, where He said:

*For I came down from heaven, not to do Mine own will, but the will of Him that sent Me. And this is the Father's will which hath sent Me, that of all which He hath given Me I should lose nothing, but should **raise it up again at the last day.** And this is the will of Him that sent Me that everyone, which seeth the Son, and believeth on Him, may have everlasting life: and **I will raise him up at the last day.***

Note it is clearly stated by Jesus that the Father's will for all which He has given Him is that He should **raise them up again the last day!** Not rapture them off to heaven! That this being "raised up again the last day" is speaking of the resurrection is clearly seen by the conversation between Martha and Jesus:

*Then said Martha unto Jesus, Lord, if thou hadst been here, my brother had not died. But I know, even now, whatsoever thou wilt ask of God, God will give it thee. Jesus said unto her, Thy brother shall rise again. Martha saith unto Him, I know that he shall rise again in **the resurrection at the last day.*** (Jo. 11:21-24)

The reason why Jesus speaks of **raising us up again** is understood when we consider the fact that all born again believers have already been raised once. This is seen in Ep. 2:4-6:

*But God, who is rich in mercy, for His great love wherewith He loved us, Even when we were **dead in sins,** hath quickened us together with Christ, (by grace ye are saved;) And hath **raised us up***

together, *and made us sit together in heavenly places in Christ Jesus.*

It is this initial being raised up; out of being dead in sins that changes our status with the Lord:

Now therefore ye are no more strangers and for-eigners, but fellow citizens with the saints and of the household of God (Ep.2:19). *For ye were sometimes darkness, but now are ye light in the Lord: walk as children of light: (For the fruit of the Spirit is in all goodness and righteousness and truth.* (Ep.5:8, 9)

While the initial "quickening" changes our status and gives us a place in the household of God, it is still required of us to walk as children of light and make our calling and election sure!

Wherefore the rather, brethren, give diligence to make your calling and election sure: for if ye do these things, ye shall never fall: For so an entrance shall be ministered unto you abun-dantly into the everlasting kingdom of our Lord and Saviour Jesus Christ. (II Pe. 1:10, 11)

The initial status and place in the household of God is given to us on the basis of the sacrificial death of Jesus on our behalf. Though we had been sold under by sin by Adam, and were, as children of darkness, dead in trespasses and sins; by the atoning work of Jesus we can receive forgiveness of our sins, be quickened from the dead, and brought forth as children of light! This is all on the basis of what Jesus accomplished by **His walk and His death** on our behalf! His walk and His death do not, however, make our calling and election sure! We still have to go on to perfection! We still have to apprehend that for which also we are apprehended of Christ Jesus, to know Him, and the power of His resurrection! We can only accomplish this by **our own walk and our own death:**

> *Know ye not, that so many of us as were baptized into Jesus Christ were baptized into His death?*
>
> *Therefore,* **we are buried with Him by baptism into death:** *that like as Christ was raised up from the dead by the glory of the Father, even* **so we also should walk in newness of life.**
>
> *For* **if we have been planted together in the likeness of His death, we shall be also in the likeness of His resurrection:**
>
> *Knowing this, that our old man is crucified with Him, that the body of sin might be destroyed, that henceforth we should not serve sin. For* **he that is dead is freed from sin.** *Now* **if we be dead with Christ,** *we believe that* **we shall also live with Him.** (Ro. 6:3-8)

Then we will not only be alive, but alive forever more! Then will death, the last enemy, be swallowed up in victory! Then will we experience the final adoption as sons, to wit, the redemption of our bodies! Then shall it appear what we shall be! Then will the time have come for the manifestation of the sons of God to all creation! Then will the creature itself be delivered from the bondage of the corruption into the glorious liberty of the sons of God! Then will the time have come for the kingdoms of this world to become the kingdoms of our Lord and His Christ! Then will come peace on earth and good will toward men!

In Heb. 6:1, 2, the apostle Paul lays out for us the foundational doctrines of the Christian faith. We read:

> *Therefore leaving the principles of the doctrine of Christ, let us go on unto **perfection;** not laying the foundation of repentance from dead works, and of faith toward God, Of the doctrine of baptisms, and of laying on of hands, and of **resurrection of the dead,** and of eternal judgment.*

We note that while the doctrine of the resurrection of the dead is included, the doctrine of the rapture is conspicuously absent!

In Heb. 6:1, the exhortation of Paul is, "let us go on to perfection!" As we have seen the clear teaching of Scripture is that perfection is realized in Christ by resurrection, not by rapture! That this is the teaching of the early church fathers is clear not only in the scriptures that we have looked at, but also in Acts 17: 16-18:

> *Now while Paul waited for them at Athens, his spirit was stirred in him, when he saw the city wholly given to idolatry. Therefore disputed he in the synagogue with the Jews, and with the devout persons, and in the market daily with them that met with him. Then certain philosophers of the Epicureans, and of the Stoics, encountered him. And some said, What will this babbler say? Others said, He seemeth to be a setter forth of strange gods: because he preached unto them Jesus, and the **resurrection.***

In Acts 24:14, 15, we read:

> *But this I confess unto thee, that after the way they call heresy, so worship I the God of my fa-*

*thers, believing all things which are written in the law and in the prophets: And have hope toward God, which they themselves also allow, that there shall be a **resurrection of the dead,** both of the just and the unjust.*

Finally in Ro. 1:3, we read that Jesus was declared to be the son of God with power, according to the spirit of holiness. How? **"By the resurrection from the dead!"**

"Now the God of peace, that brought again from the dead our Lord Jesus, that great shepherd of the sheep, through the blood of the everlasting covenant, Make you perfect in every good work to do His will, working in you that which is well pleasing in His sight, through Jesus Christ, to whom be glory for ever and ever. **Amen.**" (He. 13:20, 21)